THE

RUBLEV

TRINITY

The Icon of the Trinity

by the Monk-Painter

Andrei Rublev

GABRIEL BUNGE

The Rublev Trinity

*The Icon of the Trinity by the Monk-Painter
Andrei Rublev*

with a foreword by Sergei S. Averintsev

translation by Andrew Louth

ST VLADIMIR'S SEMINARY PRESS
CRESTWOOD, NEW YORK • 2007

Library of Congress Cataloging-in-Publication Data

Bunge, Gabriel, 1940–
      [Andere Paraklet. English]
      The Rublev Trinity : the icon of the Trinity by the monk-painter Andrei Rublev /
Gabriel Bunge ; with a foreword by Sergei S. Averintsev ; translation by Andrew Louth.
            p.   cm.
      Includes bibliographical references.
      ISBN–13: 978–0–88141–310–6 (alk. paper)
      ISBN–10: 0–88141–310–0 (alk. paper)
      1. Rublev, Andrei, Saint, d. ca. 1430. Trinity.   2. Rublev, Andrei, Saint, d. ca. 1430—
Criticism and interpretation.   3. Trinity—Art.   4. Icons—Cult—Russia.   I. Rublev,
Andrei, Saint, d. ca. 1430.   II. Title.

N8189.5.R8A77 2007
704.9'4852092—dc22

                                                                                          2006100965

© 2007

ST VLADIMIR'S SEMINARY PRESS
575 Scarsdale Rd, Crestwood, NY 10707
1–800–204–2665
www.svspress.com

Book design by Amber Schley.

ISBN 0–88141–310–0
ISBN 978–0–88141–310–6

PRINTED IN CHINA

Dedicated in love
to the venerable sons of
Saint Sergii of Radonezh

"There exists the icon of the Trinity by St Andrei Rublev; therefore, God exists."

—ST PAVEL FLORENSKY

Contents

Foreword

After the appearance of so many treatises, essays, scholarly investigations, and dreamy fantasies about that most famous of Russian icons, St Andrei Rublev's icon of the Trinity, it was, for me—a Russian and an unworthy heir to the tradition of Russian Orthodoxy—an extraordinary experience to read this book by Father Gabriel Bunge. With the publication of this book, we have, at last, a theological explanation of this much-praised icon that is detailed and comprehensive, inspired and utterly sober, and therefore "Orthodox" in the truest sense of the word.

Moreover, this work recalls the Latin proverb, *Similia similibus cognoscuntur:* "like is known only by like." The tempo of this book breathes in rhythm with the genuine spirit of Orthodox *hesychia*, which is kindred to the spirit of Benedictine *pax*, "peace." This tempo, neither fast nor slow, is completely gentle and peaceful: the cadence of recollected contemplation, of so-called spiritual activity (Russian: *umnoë delanie*). Compared to it, the conventional style of academic discourse seems hasty and precipitous. In this volume, for example, all the numerous biblical and liturgical citations are not simply referenced but quoted in their completeness, so that in reality, in the presence of contemplative activity, they may be at hand for the reader. Perhaps these same references and citations determine the rhythmic flow of the Orthodox Divine Liturgy? So it seems to me.

Again: like is known by like. Theology is a matter of knowledge, of insight, of interpretation that is also scientifically correct and precise and demonstrable because it is intellectually incontestable, not simply childish, edifying meditation. Theology is either an exact science or it is nothing. Accordingly, I would like to emphasize with approval that, from a purely scholarly point of view the whole enterprise of Fr Gabriel Bunge seems thoroughly rational. This would be so, even if, for example, all the references to ideas in patristic texts—which are so alluring, so full of meaning, and so deep—were fundamentally eliminated on the ground that knowledge of these texts in a Russian milieu by a monk-painter at the beginning of the fifteenth century is quite improbable. For, just as well-grounded is the author's understanding of the necessity for a precise and coherent theological explanation of Rublev's icon: It was precisely Russian iconographic art, much more than the Romanesque and Gothic sacred art of the West, that conceived of itself as a theologically responsible confession of faith and, indeed, was thus understood by the whole Orthodox tradition and was itself conscious of this responsibility. The monk-painters (and indeed the other monastic brothers) learnt their Orthodox faith through the prayer of the Hours and the Divine Liturgy, through the familiar texts of the hymns and the Gospel readings. It is to the content found there that the whole method of Fr Gabriel Bunge is completely attuned.

What else should I say? Should I regret that despite so many attempts from the Russian perspectives of art history, intellectual history, and even theology, nothing equal to this work has appeared? Or, quite the contrary, give rein to pure joy that the icon, which for every Russian believer expresses the palladium, the sign and meaning of Holy Russia, has been so well understood by a Western Benedictine monk, so perfectly explained? Certainly, the latter.

And now I beg forgiveness for an all-too-personal confession: When Providence granted me to get to know Fr Gabriel Bunge, not just through his works, but also face to face, I listened with admiration to his words, which not only bore witness to a genuine, inimitable love for the tradition of the Eastern Church, but also to an astonishingly pertinent understanding of the peculiarity of Russian Orthodoxy, and indeed of its situation today—as from an insider.

However, this act of understanding comes, in the genuine sense of the word, "from an outsider," and as it is attained, it overcomes any national, cultural, or confessional difference. For this reason alone, this book should be regarded as much more than a distinguished academic achievement or even a priceless spiritual lesson. Indeed, I make bold to say that this book is not only *about* Rublev's icon of the Trinity, but is also *ad intentionem*, in accordance with the prayerful intentions of the two saints Sergii of Radonezh and Andrei Rublev, which find visible expression in this icon. But their prayerful intentions were nothing less than "the union of all" (according to the Church Slavonic text of the Orthodox liturgical prayer: *soedinenie vsech*)—under the sign of the undivided Trinity. So may this book, too, become, as the icon once became, a triumph over the "hostility of the world," a comfort to all for whom the matter of the union of all lies close to their hearts; a signpost towards the goal that was named by Jesus Christ himself in the so-called High-Priestly Prayer: *ut omnes unum sint*, "that they all may be one"(Jn 17.21).

Sergei S. Averintsev
Moscow, Feast of St Basil the Great of Caesarea, 1993

Introduction

The icon of the Holy Trinity by the saint and painter-monk Andrei Rublev has at all times aroused great interest. Previous writings relate the circumstances of its genesis; a church council included it among canonical models; modern authors dedicate to it a constantly growing number of theological and art-historical investigations. The study of this secondary literature alone has become a subject in itself.[1] There can scarcely be any other icon about which so much has been written.

Anyone who endeavors to survey this lively academic engagement with Rublev's *Troitsa* (Trinity) will be astounded at the multitude of attempts to discover its meaning, which, passing from theology to sociology, scarcely leave out any area of scholarly enquiry. This aesthetic masterpiece fascinates not only believers, for whom it was originally made, but even those completely alien to religion.

The bewildering multitude of at times completely opposed meanings attributed to this image has various reasons, both internal and external. If one discounts purely subjective meanings, which attempt to subordinate the icon to purposes essentially foreign to it, then the main reason for these discrepancies lies in the fact that, on the one hand, Rublev's work is an original creation, but, on the other, forms the high point of a development that lasted more than a millennium. This makes it difficult to find the right starting point: not to take into account the more than thousand-year-old iconographic tradition—the artistic sediment of an even longer history of the interpretation of Gen 18.1–16—would miss the meaning of the icon, as would not to pay attention to those peculiarities that distinguish it from earlier icons. For, Rublev's *Troitsa* is both thoroughly traditional and, equally in an unqualified sense, unique.

Moreover, despite the apparent similarities among numerous icons of the "Hospitality of Abraham," it is not possible to speak of *the* Icon of *Philoxenia* (Hospitality). Not only has each of the principal types that emerged in the tradition its own sense, but also the individual painters themselves—before and after Rublev, and even his contemporaries—understood it in accordance with their own gifts and introduced their own nuances. However, the distinct creation of Rublev is striking.

In what follows, no attempt is made to engage with the enormous quantity of secondary literature, not least because much of what has appeared in Russia is hardly, if at all, accessible in the West.[2] Our aim is not to increase the scholarship on Rublev's icon but rather, above all, to make its timeless message accessible to the contemporary praying believer.

Additionally, several circumstances were determinative in the making of Rublev's *Troitsa* that require careful consideration: the great temporal distance of more than five hundred years that separates us from Rublev; the different religious world to which he belonged; the thousand-year iconographic tradition of

1 See the Select Bibliography. An extensive bibliography can also be found in the works of Mainka, *Rublev's Dreifaltigkeitsikone* (1986), Müller, *Dreifaltigkeitsikone*, and Vzdornov, *Dreifaltigkeit Andrej Rubljovs.*

2 I owe much to Mainka, for his survey of the patristic interpretation of Gen 18, to Müller, for his critical evaluation of the Church Slavonic sources, and to Vzdornov, for his extensive anthology of modern Russian interpretations of the icon. Valuable, too, are the nineteen coloured reproductions of details of Rublev's *Troitsa* at the beginning of his work. [Cf. Note 1—Trans.]

the Eastern Church, to which he was indebted; and the theological interpretation of the scene from Genesis that reaches back to the time of the apostles.

At the end of our efforts, it will be sufficient to grasp what St Sergii of Radonezh, according to biographical witness, was engaged in before an icon of the Holy Trinity: Spirit-filled prayer, intelligent worship of the inexhaustible mystery of the All-holy Trinity. All contemplation of icons, in accordance with a tradition reaching back to Rublev himself, should always lead from the interpretation back to what is interpreted.

In order to understand better the theological and spiritual hinterland of the iconographic tradition, we shall draw especially on the rich treasury of prayer found in the liturgical poetry of the Eastern Church. For, the icon essentially belongs to the realm of the liturgy, and liturgical verse—poetry made theology— is that part of the literary tradition, with which, next to the Scriptures, even uneducated Christians (and doubtless, such was Andrei Rublev) were most familiar. So, even if Rublev had never read any works of any of the great Fathers of the Eastern Church, as is indeed likely, the fruit of centuries-long theological meditation in the form of hymns, through the daily prayer of the Hours, would still have been accessible to him.

In image and song, in mutually complementary ways, which made present the saving deeds of God witnessed by the Scriptures, we find the key to understanding the icon of the Holy Trinity. Rublev's *Troitsa* will open to us its own meaning if we become familiar with the spiritual realm in which and for which it came into being. For this icon, like none other, is bound up with a certain historically determined situation and its impact: with Sergii of Radonezh and the Monastery of the Trinity that he founded.

CHAPTER ONE

Original and Copy

"God is Spirit," says Christ (Jn 4.24), absolute being, limited by neither time nor space. The true worshipper of the Father worships him henceforth neither on Mount Gerizim nor in Jerusalem, but in spirit and truth. Therefore, any pictured image of God, insofar as it attempts to circumscribe him, is forthwith a non-thing, what the prophets rightly called a "nothing." There are no material images of the invisible, immaterial, and incorporeal Godhead. The Old Testament prohibition against images consequently remains for the Church, as well, an enduring, binding prohibition.

Yet, the God of revelation—always directly self-revelation—is anything but a bare, abstract, impersonal principle. The One who said of himself "I am, that I am" (Ex 3.14) is, in the highest, absolute sense, personal being.

So too, it is more than just metaphorical language when the Scriptures speak of the "countenance of God," indeed even of the "image of God" (2 Cor 4.4). To be sure, this image of God is not something outside God and certainly not an image of God brought to perfection by anyone else. Rather, God bears in a mysterious way his own image *in himself*, for which reason the Fathers can equate image and countenance. This living image of God is the "only begotten Son" who is "in the bosom of the Father" (Jn 1:18).

This only begotten Son, however, "became flesh and dwelt among us, and we have seen his glory, the glory as of the only begotten of the Father, full of grace and truth" (Jn 1.14). Therefore, the Father, "whom no one has ever seen" (Jn 1.18), revealed himself in his Son, as it were, as a "countenance," in which he turns himself towards the world. He does this from the beginning of the creation, yet thanks to the Incarnation of the Only Begotten, this countenance has become visible for us. Thus, the Incarnate One says of himself: "He who has seen me has seen the Father" (Jn 14.9).

The Son, "the splendour of the glory and the express image of the substance" of the Father (Heb 1.3) and his uniquely true "exegete" (Jn 1.18) is, therefore, *as person*, the uniquely true "image of the invisible God" (Col 1.15)—the countenance of God, that vision which brings salvation to human kind (Ps 79.4ff.).

❧

Human kind is capable of apprehending this vision of the image of the invisible God, because he is himself a created "image of God's own being" (Wisd 2.23). For more exactly, the immaterial, incorporeal and formless spirit of human kind is, as the Fathers very subtly observed and very profoundly explained, created "*according* to the image of God" (Gen 1.27 LXX) and, therefore is equally "the image of the Image" (Origen), that is, the image of the Son, of the Original. For as the Son is in the Spirit one with the Father, so this created image of the Image reflects the triune being of the uncreated Godhead.

> When in the beginning you formed Adam, O Lord, then you cried to your real Word, O merciful One: "According to our image, let us make him." The Holy Spirit, too, was present as creator. Therefore we cry out to you: Our God the Creator, Glory to you.[1]

> In order to manifest the overflow of your goodness, you created human beings, limitlessly powerful Triad, the sole earthly image of your sovereign lordship, O Fashioner.[2]

❧

The Fathers saw the nature of this created "image-likeness to God" not in something static, but in a living *relationship*: the *relatedness* of the created spirit to God, the pure *receptivity* and openness of the copy to its divine original.

> You have created human kind out of goodness, and formed him in your image. Come and dwell in me, my threefold radiant God, as good and merciful.[3]

> In order to make known to human kind your unique, thrice radiant Godhead, first you fashioned human kind and formed him in your image, and gave him, O lover of human kind, intellect, reason [word] and spirit.[4]

> As you have formed me according to your image and likeness, all-working thearchic Triad, unconfused Monad, give me wisdom and light to do your holy will, which is good in power and perfect.[5]

❧

The vision of God is, therefore, a personal, immediate knowledge of God "face to face" (1 Cor 13.12) between creator and creature, the expression of the most inward, loving communion that only exists between the Father and the Son (Jn 17.3). This immediate vision is not yet possible for us in its perfection, so much so that human kind, in the words of the Psalmist, longs for it. Now, we equally see and know as it were "through a glass darkly," but then we "shall know, even as we are known" (1 Cor 13.12).

This original-copy relationship finds mystical reality, a gracious foretaste of this future glory, here on earth in that conversation (*homilia*) of the spirit with God, transcending any representation, whether in image or concept, that the masters of the spiritual life call prayer. It finds its fulness and perfection only in that ineffable communion with God, a communion at once typified (*typos*) and created by the Holy Trinity itself thanks to its own, uncreated, three-in-one being (Jn 17.21).

When, indeed, the Son, the Original, is revealed "as he is" (cf. 1 Jn 3.2), then that assimilation (*homoiōsis*) to the archetype will take place in his image (*eikōn*), to which our spirit, according to the teaching of the Fathers, has been destined since our creation (Gen 1.26), but which was not immediately conferred (Gen 1.27).

1 *Paraklitiki*, Canon for the Midnight Office, Sunday, tone 2, kathisma 1.

2 Ibid., tone 7, ode 1, troparion 2.

3 Ibid., tone 5, ode 1, troparion 1.

4 Ibid., tone 1, ode 1, troparion 2.

5 Ibid., tone 1, ode 4, troparion 4.

Human kind was, in fact, created in a process of *becoming*: on the way from image to assimilation. When, on his own authority, he sought to take this step towards being like God, then came the Fall (Gen 3). Yet "the thoughts of the heart of the Lord endure from generation to generation" (Ps 32.11), and on the tangled ways of the history of salvation, the Creator, as Redeemer and Perfecter, guides his original intention to its goal, where he finally "conforms to the image of his Son" "those whom he foreknew" (Rom 8.29).

> Wishing to deify human kind now subject to corruption, the One who through goodness formed him and made him an image of this divine form, O Virgin, assumed humanity from you and proclaimed the one, threefold Thearchy.[6]

> In order to make Adam new again, All-Pure One, his Creator came forth from you in visible human form and deified human beings, who therefore cry out: "Blessed is the fruit of your womb, All-Pure One."[7]

⚭

The Incarnation of the Son introduces into the question about the image of God a radical change, as we have seen. While it remains true that "no one has seen God at any time" (Jn 1.18), for he "dwells in unapproachable light, that no one has seen or can see" (1 Tim 6.16), it is also true that those who have beheld the glory of the Only Begotten see in him the Father.

The Fathers are at one in maintaining that only the epiphany of the incarnate God-Logos, his visible manifestation in a world of shapes and forms, establishes the presupposition for the development of an icon or image of God and, at the same time, the limits of what can be depicted.

> Being uncircumscribed in your divine nature, you thought it right, in the last times, O Master, to be circumscribed by becoming incarnate. For, through the assumption of the flesh, you assumed all its properties. Therefore, with your form imprinted on us, we greet it relatively[8] and are raised up to your love. From it we draw the grace of healing, and follow the divine traditions of the Apostles.[9]

> Raising up the copy of your flesh, O Lord, we greet it relatively, showing forth the great mystery of your Dispensation. For you did not appear to us in appearance, as the children of Mani say, who fight against God, O Friend of human kind, but, in the truth and nature of the flesh. Through it we lift up our longing and our love for you.[10]

> Invisible in his divine nature without beginning, he was seen as mortal formed from your pure blood, O Maid, through his extreme compassion. As we write down the memory of his flesh, all we the faithful venerate him with honour and reverently magnify him.[11]

⚭

6 Ibid., tone 4, ode 5, theotokion.

7 Ibid., tone 7, ode 7, theotokion.

8 "Relatively," "relative," here and elsewhere, is a reference to the notion, developed by the defenders of icons during the iconoclast controversy, of "relative veneration" (*schetikē proskynesis*), used to make clear that the veneration offered to icons is offered to them in virtue of the relationship they bear to the one depicted who thus receives this "relative" veneration; so that in venerating an icon, one is venerating the one depicted in the icon, not the material from which the icon is made—Trans.

9 *Triodion,* Sunday of Orthodoxy, Great Vespers, third sticheron.

10 Ibid., Lauds, second sticheron.

11 Ibid., Little Vespers, theotokion 1.

The icon is an image of the One who alone is in the truth—and has truly manifested himself to us in the flesh, for, "God has come visibly" (Ps 49.2 LXX). In contrast, the idols of the gods were never more that the fashionings of human vanity, for the gods of the pagans are themselves vain "nothings," without any true being.

> Beholding the crucifixion in an image, we venerate Christ with love and embrace the signs of him, and bow down to them, not honouring them as gods.[12]

> Why then, thrice-wretched one, do you hate the pure form of Christ's Incarnation and of all his saints? For we faithful do not venerate dumb idols.[13]

In the veneration of icons, human beings do not submit themselves through the idols of the gods to any godhead of their own vain imagination or empty desires, but they submit themselves rather to the tremendous reality that the only true God has in grace shown himself to the eye of faith—and only to it: to him is due all glory!

> The honour of the image, says Basil, is raised to the archetype. Therefore we venerate relatively the images of Christ the Saviour, and of all the Saints, and clinging to them, we shall never now be dragged down to impiety.[14]

Or, to use the words of a modern Orthodox theologian and saint: "An icon remembers its prototype."[15] Outside the strictly theological context of the remembering of the saving deeds of the Incarnate One, the icon sinks to the level of a mere object of art, and thus to that of a coveted collector's piece, robbed of its soul. Its meaning is now measured only by its profane artistic value, or simply by the market value it attracts in accordance with its human desirability. Robbed of its *logos* (sense, word, meaning), the icon can no longer proclaim its theological message. For, remembering and making present [a spiritual reality] for the faithful is something the icon has in common with the word that proclaims the faith.

> What the words of the sermon are for the ear, so the icons are for the eye. And this is so not because the icon conditionally "translates" some written text or other but, instead, because both icon and text have as their immediate object—a subject from which neither seeks to be separated and to the manifesting of which both essentially seek: both have as their subject the same spiritual reality.[16]

Like the Church's preaching of the word, icon painting makes use of its own principles. It consciously submits to its own rules and thus renounces much that is essential for profane painting. So, it rejects what the world considers to be the natural, or central, perspective, which issues from the standpoint of the beholder, and chooses what can be considered the unartistic reverse perspective,[17] which forces the beholder to surrender his own standpoint, his sense of distance. Likewise, neither are shapes and objects illuminated from outside, rather they have their own source of light within themselves.

12 Ibid., Canon of St Theodore the Studite, ode 5, troparion 2.

13 Ibid., troparion 4.

14 Ibid., Little Vespers, troparion 4.

15 Florensky, *Iconostasis*, p. 71.

16 Ibid., p. 153.

17 The term "reverse perspective" was coined by Fr Pavel Florensky to characterize the typical perspective of the Orthodox icon. See his article "Reverse Perspective" in Pavel Florensky, *Beyond Vision. Essays on the Perception of Art*, compiled and edited by Nicoletta Misler, translated by Wendy Salmond, London: Reaktion Books, 2002, pp. 197–272.

"He who sees me has seen the Father" is a truth that, like the confession of Christ as Lord(cf. 1 Cor 12.3), is only accessible in the Holy Spirit. The same Spirit, who, according to the words of Christ to his disciples, will "guide you into all the truth" (Jn 16.13), also opened their eyes to the hidden manifestations of the Son in the Old Testament. For the Holy Spirit shows the "word of the Lord" that came to the prophets to be the personal Logos of the Father. Rightly, the Fathers understood the manifestations of God in the Old Testament as manifestations of the Logos and interpreted the theophanies as christophanies, for the Father effects and maintains everything through the Son (Heb 1.2f.).

The Spirit of the Lord who inspired the prophets and uttered in them the word of the Lord then shows himself in the New Testament to be not only the "power of God" but also the person of the Holy Spirit. For he is that "other Paraclete," who, taking the place of the "advocate with the Father, Jesus Christ" (1 Jn 2.1), "will abide [with the disciples] for ever" (Jn 14.16). Instead of Christ, he "will teach you all things, and bring to your remembrance all that I have said to you" (Jn 14.26). For it is his task "to bear witness to me" (Jn 15.26).

Now, only a step further leads us to discover in the prefigurations (*typoi*—1 Cor 10.6, 11) of the Old Testament, the prophetic visions of Elias, Isaias, and Daniel . . . the mystery of the Holy Trinity itself.

> The sayings of the holy seers of old revealed you beforehand symbolically as the ineffable Creator of all the ages, God and Lord in three thearchic hypostases.[18]

Among these seers, Abraham takes the first place:

> You appeared of old to Abraham at the oak of Mambre, and out of mercy gave back Isaac in reward for hospitality, God in three persons, whom we now also glorify as the God of our fathers.[19]

> When you appeared to the patriarch Abraham in the form of three men, O Monad, you demonstrated the unchangeable nature of your threefold goodness and sovereignty.[20]

> In order of old clearly to unveil one Sovereignty in three persons, you appeared, my God, in the form of three men to Abraham, who hymned your unique power.[21]

For this reason, the theologian and hymnographer Metrophanes of Smyrna took care to distinguish precisely between the prophetic prefigurations of the Old Testament and their fulfilment in the New Testament.

> Seen by them of old, the Word proclaimed beforehand in a figure the Incarnation from you, O Virgin; but later, when he appeared to human kind in truth, he revealed the one Principle in three Persons.[22]

The key to understanding the Old Testament images lies hidden in the mystery of the Incarnation of the Son.

18 *Paraklitiki*, Canon of Midnight Office, Sunday, tone 4, ode 7, troparion 2.

19 Ibid., tone 3, ode 7, troparion 3.

20 Ibid., tone 4, ode 3, troparion 2.

21 Ibid., tone 5, ode 8, troparion 1.

22 Ibid., tone 4, ode 4, theotokion.

You ensnared us with your love, O most merciful Word of God, who, out of love for us, was embodied without any change and initiated us into the mystery of the one thrice-radiant Godhead. Therefore we glorify you.[23]

This careful distinction will acquire great significance for the biblical representation of the mystery of the Trinity. For the icon painters paint "the invisible Godhead, not according to its essence, but they paint and represent it according to the vision of the prophets."[24] The visit of the three men to Abraham is indeed no manifestation of the fathomless All-holy Trinity itself, but rather a prophetic vision of this mystery, which is only unveiled step by step to the faithful mind of the Church during the course of the centuries.

Thus, St Andrei Rublev's creation stands at the zenith of a long journey. It is the ripe fruit of a theological and iconographic development within the tradition of the Eastern Church that reaches back to the earliest days of Christianity. It is this journey that we are now going to trace in broad strokes.

23 Ibid., tone 3, ode 4, theotokion.

24 "Answer of the Synod to the Chancellor Ivan Viskovatyj," cited from P. Hauptmann and G. Stricker (eds.), *Die Orthodoxe Kirche in Rußland*, Göttingen 1988, p. 282.

PLATE 1

Fifth-century pilgrim
souvenir of Abraham's
three visitors.

CHAPTER TWO

The Iconographic Tradition

Pictorial representations of the visit of the three men to Abraham reach back to the beginnings of Christian iconography and in time became, especially in the Eastern Church, ever more numerous. For the first millennium, however, works are limited almost entirely to the Latin West, because in the Greek East, during the Iconoclast Controversy (730–843), countless icons were destroyed. Although few works on this subject by Greek iconographers survive, evidence for them can be seen in Western works, which followed almost completely the fashion set by the East.

✎

Ostensibly, there was already in pre-Constantinian times a painted picture (*graphē*) of Abraham's three visitors in the grove of Mambre, as the church historian Eusebios of Caesarea reports; we shall come back to this important text in a later context.[1] The picture itself, which Eusebios described in outline, is no longer extant, but there seems to be an early copy, in the form of a kind of pilgrim souvenir, which apparently dates from the fifth century (plate 1).

Whether the painting described by Eusebios—depicted on the aforementioned pilgrim souvenir, which survives as a limestone seal—is of Christian origin is subject to considerable doubt.[2] Possibly this image is a pagan-syncretistic representation that took up local, Jewish traditions about Abraham and was later interpreted by Christians in their own way. If this simple seal is really a copy of the picture at Mambre, then it allows us to form some conception of the lost original.

We recognize three youthful figures, clad in chiton (draped, belted garment) and chlamys (cloak), depicted in a frontal position. They sit behind a small, three-legged table on which can be seen what appears to be three star-shaped loaves. Each figure carries in his left hand a drinking bowl. On the left appears a tree, which leans over all three of them and from which hangs a birdcage.

At the bottom, separated from the three youths by a line, are images representing Abraham's well, a calf, a man carrying what looks like a basin, as well as a woman with a large drinking vessel. The youth on the left points with his staff at the well, the middle one raises his right hand up towards the tree, and the one on the right extends his staff to the calf.

All these elements, including the birdcage and the well, come to belong, if sometimes in a different order, to the essential components of the iconographic tradition. The drinking bowls, for example, will later stand on the table; the hosts, Abraham and Sarah, will appear in their full size, not separated from their guests; and so forth. The strict frontal posture of the three visitors, always depicted as youths, will be maintained for centuries until the post-iconoclastic period, when

1 See the Excursus, pp. 113–114.

2 See the Excursus.

PLATE 2

Oldest depiction of
Genesis 18; fresco, Via
Latina Catacomb, first
half of the fourth century.

they are placed in another position. The absence of Abraham's tent in the fifth-century copy is surprising. This element, depicted as a house, is included in all of the definitely Christian depictions, insofar as it represents the entertainment of the guests.

∽

The earliest Christian depiction of Gen 18, as far as we are aware, is a fresco, unique among its kind, from the catacombs discovered in 1955 on the Via Latina, one of the important roads of ancient Rome (plate 2: first half of the fourth century). It shows a bearded Abraham sitting under a terebinth,[3] with three youths in white garments standing before him on the right, on a raised circular platform. Abraham greets the approaching youths with his raised right hand, while they respond with the same gesture. Also on Abraham's right, one can see the calf, which refers to the not-yet-represented hospitality.

3 A small tree (*Pistacia
terbinthus*), native to the
Mediterranean region,
yielding turpentine and
noted for its aromatic and
medicinal resin—Trans.

24

Apart from the calf, which is, however, not depicted without a purpose, we have an exact reproduction of Gen 18.1–2a: Abraham sits at his midday meal under the terebinth of Mambre and raises his eyes to see three men "standing over against him," as it is literally in the text of the Septuagint—a detail that concerned many a church father and gave rise to profound explanations.

Yet, this early fresco is anything but a naïve illustrated narrative of an Old Testament event. One notices this straightaway if one compares this depiction more closely with the scriptural text. Within the text, first of all, is the matter of God's visit to Abraham, then of three men, whom the forefather saw. At the end, the text says that the Lord went away from Abraham (Gen 18.33), while the two angels went down to Sodom alone (Gen 19.1).

In the fresco, instead of three men there appear three almost childlike youths. Nothing indicates that one of them is the Lord. Nor are the two angels expressly designated as such; that is, they have neither halo nor wings nor messenger staves. In fact, though, these requisites are quite dispensable in the early period. Angels are mostly, though not exclusively, represented as beardless youths in white garments.[4] Even the divine Logos is normally represented as a beardless youth, often designated as such by a scroll in his left hand.

Surprisingly, and significant for the interpretation of the fresco, Abraham's three visitors are completely similar to one another in size (that the middle one is a bit shorter is scarcely noticeable), in clothing, and above, all in gesture. Strangely, and clearly noticeable, the three youths, who are already raised up from their surroundings by the circular elevation on which they are standing, are also drawn close together, thus further strengthening the impression of their unity.

Clearly, in this fresco there is already interpretation and not simply a reproduction of the biblical account. But what did the painter want to depict? The Lord, that is, the Logos, in the company of two angels? Or, rather, three angels in the form of three youthful, male forms? Whatever the intent, this fresco is without parallel among the catacomb paintings, so much so that we wonder what meaning it had in this very special context.

The treatment of this theme in the following century comes in the form of a magnificent mosaic from Santa Maria Maggiore in Rome (plate 3: first half of the fifth century). It combines several scenes in a single picture, something we find in many later depictions. At the top, Abraham bends down on his knees to greet the approaching guests; thus, Gen 18.2b is here depicted. Again, there appear three white-clad, beardless youths. They now have *nimbi*,[5] as is typical in antiquity for divine beings, deified humans, and allegorical figures. What is clearly different is the central figure completely enclosed in a *mandorla*, something that clearly distinguishes him from the accompanying figures.

At the bottom, on the left, the preparation of the reception is depicted. Abraham's tent is recognizable in the form of a house, with Sarah in front of it preparing the loaves, and Abraham giving her instructions. Here, then, Gen 18.6 is depicted. On the right of the picture, the reception proper is taking place. The three youths sit side by side behind a right-angled table, which is not mentioned

4 Cf. the different accounts of the Resurrection: Mk 16.5 (youth in white garment), Mt 28.2 (an angel), Lk 24.4 (two men).

5 A "nimbus" is a pictorial indication of radiant light or glory about the head of each of the angels—Trans.

PLATE 3

Mosaic from Santa Maria
Maggiore, Rome; first half
of fifth century.

in the scriptural text. In front of the table, a great ewer stands for washing (cf. Gen 18.4). Three loaves are on the table (Gen 18.6 mentions three measures of meal, from which Sarah baked three loaves). On the left stands Abraham, in the shadow of the terebinth, offering his guests the calf—whole!—on a dish.

In contrast to the upper scene, the three youths are not distinguished one from another; that the one on the right has somewhat shorter hair is scarcely

26

IEREMIA

PLATE 4

Mosaic from San Vitale, Ravenna; before AD 547.

significant. Their clothing again is completely the same; it is only their gestures that are different. The youth on the left holds his hand in blessing, turning towards the middle figure, who points to the calf, while the figure on the right points with his finger to the bread. In these ways, a complete network of relationships becomes visible. Clearly, the focus of the scene is the central figure, the calf, and the loaves. Again, the representation of this scene is not a simple narrative depiction. Rather, the picture as a whole is informed by an interpretation of the biblical event that has been thoroughly thought through.

※

Such careful interpretation is still more clearly apparent in our next example, the great mosaic from San Vitale in Ravenna, Italy (plate 4: before AD 547). As with the S. Maria mosaic, several scenes are united in a single picture. To the left, Sarah is recognizable standing in the opening of the door, doubtful about the promised birth of Isaac (cf. Gen 18.12); in the middle there is the entertainment of the three men; on the right is added the sacrifice of Isaac, from a much later narrative context. The obviously intentional typological meaning of this grouping is made perfectly clear by the placement of the mosaic in relationship to the whole pictorial programme in the church space. The mosaic is located in the altar area of the church, and on the opposite wall, as a counterpart, are depictions of the sacrifices of Abel and Melchisedec, united in a single picture. On an altar with costly coverings, Abel brings a lamb, and Melchisedec offers three round loaves and a great

27

two-handled chalice. The Old Testament scenes of sacrifice are therefore quite clearly to be understood as "types" or "figures" of the New Testament sacrificial meal of the Eucharist. At the centre stands Christ, who, according to the Epistle to the Hebrews, is both simultaneously the sacrifice and the priest: prefigured in Abel (cf. Heb 12.24), Melchisedec (Heb *passim*), and Isaac (Heb 11.19).

The pictorial programme as a whole does not, however, exclude the possibility that the depiction of Abraham's visitors has its own meaning, over and above this typological reference. Here, too, the three youths are almost completely equal one to another, even as far as gesture. The central figure and the one on the right are blessing with their right hands, while those on the left and the right point to the three disc-shaped loaves, each marked with an X, in this way directing particular attention to them. As in S. Maria Maggiore, Abraham brings his guests a whole calf on a dish (in later icons, there appears a table on which stands a vessel, containing a calf's head).

28

❧

These four paintings and mosaics are, as far as I am aware, the only extant witnesses from the first millennium. Despite the small number, they clearly attest to the most ancient iconographic type: correctly designated, independently of any possible typological meaning, as a depiction of the hospitality of Abraham, for it reproduces something essentially faithful to the biblical account. The three guests, along with Abraham and Sarah (when they are depicted at all), are integral elements of the composition.

From the earliest depictions, the three visitors appear as beardless youths in white garments. However, there are some distinctions. In S. Maria Maggiore and S. Vitale, they have also simple nimbi; it is in this form that angels mostly appear in the early Christian period (in the case of New Testament scenes, they also have wings, as does the youthful God–Logos). And, although the almost perfect equality of the three visitors is striking, despite their equality, we learn that there is a difference among them, as the scene of greeting at S. Maria Maggiore shows us: in contrast to the catacomb on the Via Latina, the central figure is designated as the Lord.

❧

In its basic conception, this iconographical type remained almost unchanged throughout many centuries, as a glance at the Norman mosaics of Sicily discloses. Our first example comes from the Cappella Palatina at the Norman Palace in Palermo (plate 5: twelfth century). The greeting of the guests, who now have both wings and messenger's staves, and their entertainment are again united in the depiction. In both posture and gesture, the three angels are almost identical. One of the angels—the one on the left in the scene of greeting and the central figure in the reception scene—has a nimbus with a red outline, which slightly distinguishes him from the other two. In the reception scene, he is the only one turned to face the beholder. This most likely is intentional, for we see the same restrained prominence of the central angel in the mosaics of S. Maria Maggiore and S. Vitale.

What is new here is the inscription. Above the scene of greeting, we read: "Abraham sees three angels and adores one,"[6] and over the scene of reception: "Abraham received the three angels as guests."[7]

Somewhat later is the mosaic in the cathedral of Monreale (plate 6: end of the twelfth century). The greeting and the reception have become separated as two scenes. In the reception scene, Sarah also appears in the open door of the tent. The three angels are again strikingly similar. Here, too, the central angel at the scene of the reception has a nimbus with a red outline. That this is no mere chance is evident from the fact that he now carries in his left hand not a staff—as in the scene of greeting—but a *scroll!* The meaning is simple: here, as in the reception scene at S. Maria Maggiore, it is made clear—only by other means, i.e., a scroll instead of a mandorla—that one of Abraham's three visitors was the "Lord."

Here, too, the picture bears an inscription. Above the scene of greeting, we read: "Abraham receives the angels as guests, and while he sees three, he adores one";[8] in contrast, over the scene of reception, we read: "Abraham ministers to angels."[9]

6 ABRAHAM S ANGELOS VIDIT ET UNUM ADORAVIT. The "s" would normally be read as SANCTOS, but the context and the similar inscription at Monreale lead us to read it as TRES.

7 ABRAHAM TRES ANGELOS HOSPITIO RECEPIT.

8 ABRAHAM ANGELOS HOSPITIO SUSCEPIT ETCUM TRES VIESIT (*sic*) UNUM ADORABIS (*sic*).

9 ABRAHAM MINISTRAT ANGELI[S].

PLATE 6

Mosaic from the cathedral of Monreale; end of twelfth/beginning of thirteenth century.

PLATE 7

Mosaic from San Marco in Venice; thirteenth century

As a final example, let us take a mosaic from San Marco in Venice (plate 7: thirteenth century). Here, again, the greeting and the reception are united in a single picture. Both scenes clearly interpret the three angels in the same way. As with the other mosaics, the three angels are depicted each with the same gesture, though the two groups of angels have different postures. On the table, as at Monreale, there is a great dish-shaped vessel, and in the background, at the entrance to the tent, stands the doubting Sarah. The long biblical inscription quotes Gen 18.1–3 and 18.8–10 (promise of the birth of Isaac) and therefore disclaims any straightforward interpretation of the scene. As with the two Sicilian depictions, this mosaic belongs to a cycle of depictions dealing with the whole life of Abraham.

If we compare these twelfth-/thirteenth-century mosaics with their predecessors from the fifth/sixth centuries, we see that all three of Abraham's visitors are clearly designated as angels by their wings. The message of the inscriptions makes it clear that this is either the artist's intention, or the one who gave the commission. Yet, these inscriptions also make it clear that the three visitors are not to be understood as just angels. Here, a tension between form and content becomes apparent—something that we have yet to investigate.

❧

10 The particular circum-
stances that led to the
creation of this type will
be discussed in the next
chapter.

While the last three mosaics belong certainly to the Latin Church of the West,
their iconography was strongly influenced by the Byzantine East, even if their
artists were not Greek. In the East, a new iconographic type had appeared around
the year 1000, as far as our evidence shows, which was destined to have an influ-
ential future. It emerged at almost the same time at far-distant corners of the cultural realm of Byzantium and must, therefore, have developed somewhat earlier.[10]

The newly awakened interest in this theme is witnessed to by the manifold uses to which this subject is suddenly put.[11] It is found not only on church walls, but also on altar screens (Georgia), seals, and in manuscripts—and not only in manuscripts of Genesis, illustrating the text of Gen 18, but also in Psalters and even in manuscripts of the Liturgy of St John Chrysostom.[12]

Let us look at an example that illustrates the attributes of this new style: a miniature from a Greek Psalter of the eleventh century (plate 8). The elements of the depiction are recognizable, certainly in their essentials—the richly bedecked table, the three angels, the doubting Sarah at the door, Abraham with his gifts, the calf in the foreground—yet, everything is different. The guests no longer sit side by side behind a rectangular table but are now often grouped round a semicircular table. The tendency to distinguish the middle angel from the others by different attributes, which we have already noticed, is further strengthened: the central angel is frequently larger than the others; the colour of his clothing is characteristically different; he alone carries a scroll in his left hand, while his right hand is raised in blessing; he alone has a nimbus with a cross; and later, in many cases the inscription "IC XC," the Greek abbreviation for Jesus Christ, further identifies him. His two companions come to be depicted in a thoroughly traditional way as heavenly messengers, that is, without personal distinguishing facial features. Often they even wear, as on a fresco from Patmos (end of the twelfth century), white garments in the ancient manner.[13] In most instances, they are nearly identical to one another.

Very frequently, if not without exception, depictions of this type now for the first time bear the title "The Holy Trinity." Moreover, the Psalter miniature under discussion is found opposite verse 13 of Psalm 49: "Am I to eat the flesh of bulls?" The Trinitarian title, as well as the manifold uses of the subject, indicates that an obvious change has taken place. The theme of the hospitality of Abraham has been freed from its immediate Old Testament context (Abraham cycle) and begins to take on a life of its own. While the mosaics in Sicily are part of a comprehensive Old Testament pictorial programme, they show elements that reflect this new type (Monreale).

The historical background responsible for creating this emergent type will be discussed in the next chapter; here we shall simply note that the so-called Iconoclast Controversy occurred in the period between the mosaic from S. Vitale (sixth century) and the advent of the new type (about the tenth century).

❧

Because of the lively exchange that took place between the Byzantine and the Slavic realms, we very quickly encounter this new Byzantine iconographical type in Russia as well. A particularly fine and pure example is displayed on the bronze south doors of the Church of the Nativity of the Virgin in Suzdal (plate 9: circa 1230). The central angel alone has a cross nimbus and holds a scroll in his left hand, while the other two angels hold in their left hands messenger staves. Three loaves

11 See numerous examples in Vzdornov, *Dreifaltigkeit Andrej Rubljovs.*

12 Cf. Grabar "Un rouleau liturgique constantinopolitain," p. 175 (fig. 15) and 187f., where further examples of the early diffusion of the subject in the Slavic realm are listed. On the placing of the miniature of the Trinity, see p. 106.

13 Cf. Papadopoulos, *Monastery of St John,* figure 6.

PLATE 9

South doors of the Church of the Nativity of the Virgin, Suzdal; about 1230.

and three chalices are placed on the table, with the central chalice clearly larger and in the form of a chalice with a paten laid on the top, suggestive of an influence from the Latin West. Significant, too, are the gestures of the three angels. The one in the middle blesses the table, the one on the left points to the chalice, and the one on the right blesses one of the three loaves. The title—half Greek, half Slavonic—reads: "Holy Trinity." Other similar examples can be found on the west doors of the same church in Suzdal (also about 1230), and in two churches in Alexandrovo near Moscow (from Novgorod, 1336 and from Tver, mid-fourteenth century).

The hinged lids of the *panagias* (icons worn by bishops) of the fourteenth to the sixteenth centuries constitute another interesting group; on the insides are often engraved a depiction of the Holy Trinity. The central angel is identified with Christ, almost always by a cross nimbus, and often also by the inscription IC XC.[14]

❧

This innovative Byzantine style of iconography was, therefore, well known in Russia before the time of Rublev. A particularly pure example—and moreover important for us, since Rublev most likely knew it—is a fresco by his teacher, Feofan Grek (Theophanes the Greek), in the church of the Transfiguration of Christ in Novgorod (plate 10: 1378). The damaged painting depicts the three angels sitting at an altar table, which has the semicircular form more frequently encountered in the East. In the middle of the *mensa*,[15] there is a large dish-shaped vessel, already familiar to us, containing the head of a calf, and beside it sit two loaves and pieces of cutlery. In the foreground, Sarah approaches from the right with the third loaf of bread, while Abraham, who must have been depicted on the left-hand side of the picture, no longer survives because of the damage to the fresco. Notice the opening in the side of the altar table facing the beholder.

The depiction of the angels is very impressive. The central one is, as often in icons of this type, clearly bigger than the other two. His raised-up form, with enormous, outstretched wings that at once overshadow and embrace the two other angels, dominates the painted scene. He bears a cross nimbus, and carries, in addition to his staff, a large scroll in his left hand. Without a doubt, this central angel symbolizes Christ, accompanied by two divine messengers.

❧

Feofan was Greek, yet the Russian masters of Rublev's time, such as the painter of the freestanding *Troitsa* from Novgorod, also took up this new style (plate 11). This *Troitsa* comes from the first half of the fifteenth century, the same period in which Rublev was painting his own, quite different Trinity.

The area of the Novgorod *Troitsa* is divided into four parts, a stylistic element that became very popular in Russia. The composition is the same as that of Feofan Grek. Here, too, the middle angel completely dominates the picture. Clothing (as in the Greek Psalter of the eleventh century, see plate 8), scroll, cross nimbus—this time with the inscribed words *ho ōn*, "He who is"—identify him as the *Kyrios*, Christ the Lord. The title, on the other hand, declares this depiction to be "Holy Trinity."

14 See information in Vzdornov, *Dreifaltigkeit Andrej Rubljovs*. Cf. also Saltykov, "Fragen der kirchlichen Kunst," esp. pp. 84f., where a hinged-lid panagia (fig. 7) is depicted.

15 Latin: a technical word for an altar table—Trans.

PLATE 10

Fresco by Feofan Grek in the Church of the Transfiguration of Christ, Novgorod; 1378.

PLATE 11
Freestanding icon, Church of St George, Novgorod; first half of the fifteenth century.

Still, this new iconographic style does not always appear in its purest form. Often, the attributes that were originally the unique prerogatives of the central angel are transferred to the other two as well. There is an example of this in a fresco of the twelfth/thirteenth century from Göreme in Cappadocia (plate 12: Asia Minor).

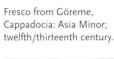

PLATE 12

Fresco from Göreme, Cappadocia: Asia Minor; twelfth/thirteenth century.

The composition is familiar, but all three angels bear a cross nimbus and hold a scroll in their left hands. Only the central angel, however, has the inscription IC XC; still, one can find icons in which this formerly unique attribute of the central angel is likewise found on all three figures. Icons of this type were known in Russia, as we shall soon see. In this Cappadocian fresco, clearly an attempt was made to remove the contradiction between a formally christological interpretation of the picture and the Trinitarian understanding implied by the title, in favour of the latter.

In the late Byzantine period, yet a third iconographical type appeared, which was destined for an equally great future. From a stylistic point of view, it not only further developed the second type, but also revealed some different characteristics. A fine example of this type is a beautiful icon from the Athonite monastery of Vatopedi (plate 13: end of the fourteenth century). Three angels sit around a rectangular, richly decorated table. The frontal view of the old mosaics, which the second iconographic type had already abandoned in the case of the two angels at the side, is now changed with regard to the central angel. He appears slightly turned to one side, yet with his inclined head, he still looks straight at the beholder. His hand is no longer raised in blessing but rather indicates with a benedictory gesture the vessel standing in front of him.

The central angel in many icons of this type bears a cross nimbus, sometimes containing the inscribed words "He who is"; at times, a superscription "IC XC" outside the nimbus serves as further identification. It is not certain whether the clear designation of the central angel as Christ derives directly from the second iconographic type (which certainly came to influence this third type), or whether

PLATE 13

Icon from Athonite monastery of Vatopedi; end of fourteenth century.

this came in at a later date. In favour of the latter supposition, we mention the freestanding icon in the Benaki Museum in Athens, in which the middle angel is not at all distinguished from the other two (plate 14: fourteenth century). All three angels are alike, especially in the colour of their garments, to such an extent that they can scarcely be distinguished one from another by their gesture and posture.

Moreover, in the Vatopedi icon the two angels at the side deserve attention. They now appear as more than simply accompanying figures. Their gestures are very lively and individual: while the one on the left blesses the table, or what is on it, the one on the right reaches out for a piece of bread, or whatever is in the vessel in front of him. The hosts Abraham and Sarah appear inserted between the angels, no longer standing before them; they bring their gifts in an attitude of reverence.

Finally, worth noticing in icons from this late Byzantine period is the background formation. Hitherto, the components have been determined by the biblical account (a house, a tree, and, eventually, a rock); now we find an often richly developed architectural setting, as seen in the icon from the Monastery of Vatopedi, even when using the ancient style of central perspective. Such changes in the background and in the presentation of the angels make clear that there has been a change of emphasis.

PLATE 14

Icon from the Benaki Museum in Athens; fourteenth century.

Examples of this style can still be found in Russian museums today (cf. plate
15).[16] In the fourteenth and fifteenth centuries, this style must have seemed very
modern. However, a glance at these works show that if Rublev had seen examples
of this late Byzantine type, he was indebted to it only in incidental details.

❧

Nevertheless, one Russian icon of this late Byzantine style is of particular interest
to us because Rublev certainly knew of it. It consists of a large board (161 x 122
cm), which probably came from the wooden church erected in St Sergii's Trinity
Monastery by Nikon, the successor of the founding abbot (plate 16). When Nikon
built his stone church in 1423–4, this little wooden church, together with its
iconostasis, was removed to the east side of the new building. The wooden church
must finally have given way to a further stone building in 1476–7. The Trinity icon
just mentioned therefore occupied different places in the monastery until 1954,
when it was transferred to the Sergiev Posad State History and Art Museum-
Reserve.

In contrast to many Greek and Russian icons of this type, this Trinity icon (c.
1411) is, like Rublev's, painted on a much larger scale. The gestures of the three
angels are determined, as in earlier Greek examples, by the object (a chalice)
placed in front of each of them. The central angel leans slightly to the left and yet
looks, not at the beholder as in the Greek examples, but at the angel on the left, as
is the case with Rublev's icon. Instead of the complex architectural scene characteristic of icons of this type, we find here only a cliff, a tree, and a house. Rublev
interchanges the house and the cliff. This at once impressive and expressive icon
represents without doubt the last, most important stage before Rublev's creation.

16 Cf. a further example
in Vzdornov, *Dreifaltigkeit
Andrej Rubljovs*, no 34,
reproduced also in W.
Felicetti-Liebenfels,
*Geschichte der byzantinis-
chen Ikonenmalerei*, Lau-
sanne: Olten, 1956, p. 136.

40

In retrospect, we can discern a line of iconographic development. The Byzantine iconographic tradition had, in the representation of Gen 18, developed two principal types in the first millennium. To review these types we will look primarily at the representation of the three angels.

In the first type, the three forms, always depicted in a frontal position, are not distinguished from each other in any way. Indeed, they often seem interchangeable. This is clearly a matter of interpretation, for the biblical text gives it no support. From the beginning, Abraham's three guests are considered angels, understood as God's messengers, although early icons hardly make this clear when depicting them as beardless youths in white clothing—something one would never gather from the biblical text. Only gradually are they depicted with nimbi, wings, and staves. Since the early renditions always formed part of the Old Testament pictorial programme of a church, these angels were understated. The emphasis was not on the angels but on a Christian-typological understanding of the Genesis event. Only with the inscriptions of the (post-iconoclast) Sicilian mosaics is this reserve abandoned.

PLATE 16

Russian icon from Trinity-St Sergii Lavra, Museum Sergiev Posad; beginning of the fifteenth century.

About the year 1000, a second type (though with roots more ancient than that period) emerges. This style is found in the upper scene of the mosaic in S. Maria Maggiore. Here one of the three guests of Abraham, now always depicted as angels (with wings), and without exception the central one, is clearly distinguished from the other two by a changing number of attributes (cross nimbus, scroll, inscription IC XC, and often by size or the colour of the clothing). In accordance with the biblical text as Christians had become accustomed to reading it, this central angel therefore symbolizes the Lord, that is, Christ. His distinctive position is further emphasized by the other two angel-figures, who now sit to the right and left of a four-cornered or semicircular table, no longer sharing the frontal view with the central figure.

These differences in the three angel figures—along with the fact

41

that most icons of this type no longer appear as part of an overall Old Testament pictorial programme but as individual pictures—clearly show a change in the understanding of Gen 18: What is new in the interpretation of Gen 18 is evident in the addition of the title "The Holy Trinity," in contrast to the former christological representation.

In the late Byzantine period, this second type is subject to a further consistent development: as the central angel surrenders its frontal view, a visible change, an alteration in the relationship of the three figures occurs. In many icons an intentional assimilation of the three angels is carried so far that they can scarcely be distinguished by either gesture or posture. This consciously intended assimilation is is manifest from other icons of this period, which transfer more or less completely the attributes formerly assigned to the central angel to the other two.

No less expressive are the changes that affect the other elements in the composition of the scene. Abraham and Sarah certainly never vanish, but their position in the picture changes. This is seen most clearly in the case of Sarah. In the first two types, we find her at the door of the house, in correspondence with the biblical account; in the third, she appears together with Abraham serving the three honoured guests. The form of the table changes as well—four-cornered, rectangular, or semicircular, yet always richly decorated and bearing all sorts of tableware. Finally, the background, which for a long time contained biblical elements, such as a tree, a house, and (often) a rock, with the third type yields to a complex architectural structure.

∞

At the end of this thoroughly consistent and discernible line of development, there emerges, so designated, an icon of the Holy Trinity. If one of the three figures is distinguished from the others, this is done in a restrained way, by a varying number of attributes that, as in the early period, identify this figure as the Lord, Christ. Without exception, it is the central angel who is thus marked out.

∞

In view of these iconographic developments, one cannot but be amazed at the unquestioning confidence with which modern authors, first in Russia, and then also in the West, have tried to identify in different ways all three angels in Rublev's icon and bring them into correspondence with the three divine persons. As proof of such an attempt, antedating Rublev, to identify the figures, the so-called Zyrian Trinity is often nowadays cited (plate 17: late fourteenth century).[17]

This icon dates back to the great missionary of the Zyrians and friend of St Sergii of Radonezh, St Stephen of Perm. It belongs to the third, late Byzantine type, and all three angels exhibit the attributes that once were given only to the central angel. Noteworthy is the Zyrian inscription over the three angels that, according to a widespread view, appears to identify unmistakeably each of the three figures. It reads: "The Father" (lost in restoration), "And the Son and the Spirit." "The Father" relates (according to N. A. Dëmina[18]) to the central angel; "And the Son" refers to the angel on the left; "And the Spirit" corresponds to the angel on the right.

17 For details, see Dëmina, *Andrei Rublev and the Painters of His Circle,* pp. 62f., and Müller, *Dreifaltigkeitsikone,* pp. 31f. and 92f.

18 N. A. Dëmina is the author of the book in the bibliography: *Andrei Rublev and the Painters of His Circle* (in Russian), Moscow 1972—Trans.

PLATE 17

Zyrian Trinity, Church of the Trinity, Vozhemsk; late fourteenth century.

At first glance, apportioning names to the three persons appears to be an amazing development in view of such a consistent iconographic tradition. A closer examination, however, reveals that the three parts of the inscription do not appear immediately above the three allegedly corresponding figures, but all together in the middle. The purpose of the inscription, then, can scarcely be to identify the three almost identical figures, but rather, to make the recently converted Zyrians mindful that these three angels symbolize the Holy Trinity and that the abstract word "Trinity" means the persons of Father, Son, and Holy Spirit.

This conclusion helps us to understand the *panagias* described on page 34. On these icons, the inscription "Holy Trinity" appears along with the words "Father, Son and Holy Spirit," without any discernible intention of identifying any of the angelic figures. Simply, the persons of the Trinity are called by their names, for the inscription round the rim reads: "Great is the name of the holy, consubstantial and undivided Trinity of the Father, the Son and the Holy Spirit."[19]

<hr />

19 Vzdornov, *Dreifaltigkeit Andrej Rubljovs*, figure 18 (fourteenth century). The central angel bears a cross nimbus with the inscribed words "He who is."

Although the iconographic tradition did not embrace the identification of each particular angel, we are, nevertheless, convinced that St Andrei Rublev, and he alone, wanted to relate each angel in his Trinity to one of the three divine persons. However, this is not obvious and needs justification; for, if this is so, then Rublev abandoned a more than thousand-year-old tradition. Thus, we need to establish what could have moved him to such a divergence.

CHAPTER THREE

The Theological Interpretation

As we have seen, Christian iconographers very quickly took up the subject of the "Hospitality of Abraham" and in the course of the centuries made various depictions of it. Alongside this was an even longer history of theological interpretation. In this chapter, we will consider the three independent theological approaches to the interpretation of Gen 18 that apparently arose during the first millennium—angelological, christological, and Trinitarian.[1]

However, attempts to relate these different interpretations to the surviving contemporary iconographic witnesses give rise to certain questions. First, what kind of a relationship is there between theology and iconography? Does theology come first? Does iconography only represent in pictorial form what has already been worked out theologically? Or, did the two develop independently of each other: iconography drawing on the general faith of the Church, understood in a traditional or intuitive way; and theology attempting an intellectual understanding, even in much later circumstances and in quite a different manner? Consider the theological discussion over the consubstantiality of the Holy Spirit in the fourth century and the theologian St Basil the Great's reference (in his *De Spiritu Sancto*) to the Church's tradition, reaching back to apostolic times yet never fixed in writing. Theology and iconography can, therefore, only be cautiously regarded as parallel.

Further, the character of the iconographic witnesses themselves present difficulties. Seldom do they have one meaning. At least three levels of meaning need to be distinguished. First, the factual meaning, in this case, the pictorial representation of Gen 18:1: This Old Testament-historical meaning corresponds to the literal sense of patristic exegesis. Christian iconography, however, is never simply illustration which means no more than the depiction.

From this factual level, we must distinguish the Christian meanings that the Church has come to see in this biblical event. This typological level of meaning, according to which an Old Testament event is understood as the type (image, figure, sketch) of the New Testament fulfilment, is, in our case, christological or Trinitarian.

Lastly, a third level of meaning, comparable to the moral meaning of Scripture, can be derived from the particular context in which a representation of Gen 18:1ff. appears; that is, as part of the larger iconographical programme of a church and from its particular location in an ecclesiastical building. This changing relationship between the icon and its liturgical and architectural setting adds a particular accent to the second level of meaning, which can be designated as the spiritual, or mystical, meaning of the picture, certainly in the sense of an interiorization of the saving truth that first radiated from the depicted event. The typological and spiritual meanings obviously do not exclude but, rather, complement each other.

1 For the following, see especially Mainka, "Rublevs Dreifaltigkeitsikone," (1962) and, for the Slav realm, also Müller, *Dreifaltigkeitsikone*, pp. 52ff.

A final difficulty arises from the complex relationship that exists between the content and its particular iconographical form. On close consideration, the iconography of Gen 18 proves to be astonishingly conservative. Forms once developed certainly become modified and also combined in the course of time, but otherwise, they are handed down unchanged, even though they are clearly no longer in accord with their particular content. Thus, a representation can be formally angelological (all three of Abraham's visitors depicted as angels) and christological (one of the three characterized as a type of Christ through certain attributes), and yet, so far as content is concerned, the inscription or title can declare it to be clearly Trinitarian. For such reasons, it is seldom easy to establish what the artist primarily wanted to depict, not to mention that the chosen iconographic form has its own meaning and so can proclaim yet another message.

❧

The earliest witness to a Christian attempt to deal with Gen 18.1ff. is found within the New Testament canon. In the letter to the Hebrews, we read: "Do not neglect to show hospitality to strangers, for thereby some have entertained angels unawares" (Heb 13.2). For the host who treats his guests in ignorance of their identity, one thinks of Abraham. The author of the letter has thus designated the visitors as angels (*angeloi*), God's messengers. If one wants to keep strictly to the biblical text, with which the author of the letter to the Hebrews was probably very familiar, then perhaps one should think of Lot, who, according to Gen 19.1ff., actually gave lodging to the two angels, while the Lord himself did not go down to Sodom (Gen 18.33).

Similarly, the Jewish biblical scholar Trypho, whose interpretation St Justin (†165) cites, quite clearly understood Abraham's visitors as angels.[2] He does this from a polemical perspective, to keep from God any anthropomorphism and also thereby to protect the biblical text. The same angelological interpretation of Gen 18 is to be found later in St Clement of Alexandria and other Fathers of the Church, and it continued for quite some time.[3]

❧

2 Justin, *Dialogue with Trypho* 56.5.

3 Clement of Alexandria, *Strom.* IV.123.1. Evagrios Pontikos (†399), who also knows the christological interpretation (see below), often introduces in his Scholia on the Psalms the angelological interpretation. Cf., too, the variant "angel" instead of "man" in one of Romanos the Melodist's kontakia (sixth century): see below, n. 9.

4 Cf. Stützer, *Kunst der römischen Katakomben,* coloured figure 35.

The search for iconographic witnesses to this angelological interpretation can be puzzling. For the more clearly the three visitors of Abraham are characterized as angels, the more certain it is, thanks to the title or inscription, that the interpretation of the representation is not angelological. For example, let us examine the oldest witness from the beginning of the fourth century.

On the fresco from the catacomb on the Via Latina (plate 2), Abraham's three visitors are depicted as beardless youths in white garments without aureoles. They are similar to the angels on Jacob's Ladder in another fresco in the same catacomb. In fact, angels, especially in the early period, are consistently represented as beardless youths with wings, although it is only in the catacomb on the Via Latina that bearded angels appear (in the portion representing the story of Balaam's ass).[4]

Abraham's three visitors are, therefore, understood as angels; the representation is formally angelological. But, is it also meant angelologically so far as the content is concerned? That is, should the three figures be understood as angels and only as angels? Probably not. The figures are almost completely the same, something which cannot be ascertained from the biblical text. For ages, the three-fold repetition of a particular symbol or letter has been a favourite stylistic means for representing the holy threeness, perfectly indistinguishable within itself.[5] If Abraham's three visitors are understood as a type of the Trinity, then, this would suggest, from the fact that the biblical text first of all speaks of "three men," a representation of three similar young men. On the typological level, we have here, therefore, an early representation of the Holy Trinity. The proper, and hitherto unique, context (catacomb), in which the fresco is found, points to a further spiritual (or mystical) dimension of the picture. Abraham himself appears here, in reference to Heb 11.12, 17–19, as an embodiment of the Christian faith in the resurrection of the dead as the work of the triune God.

The fresco from the catacomb on the Via Latina represents an iconographical type that is certainly formally angelological, yet in terms of content is to be understood as Trinitarian. The conclusion is obvious: that this angelological form makes reference to the existence of representations also in content angelological, which are perhaps of Jewish origin. To my knowledge, there are no Christian iconographical examples. The pilgrim souvenir from Mambre, which on account of its inscription is doubtless to be understood angelologically, is, as we have seen, hardly genuinely Christian, but rather of pagan-syncretistic origin.

Similarly, the iconographic type here manifest for the first time becomes with slight variants a fixed ingredient in representations of Gen 18. In the fifth and sixth centuries, the three angels already have aureoles and (so far as evidence goes) from the eleventh century also wings and staves. None of these representations, however, is to be understood angelologically in terms of content. Nothing shows this more clearly perhaps that the example from Monreale. Formally, this mosaic is designated as angelological-christological, for all three of Abraham's visitors are depicted as angels, while the middle one is additionally characterized as the Logos by a scroll. Over the scene of the reception, we read: "Abraham ministers to angels," probably a reference to Heb 13.2. But, over the scene of greeting, it says: "Abraham receives the angels as guests, and while he sees three, he adores one"—probably a reference to a famous remark of Ss Augustine or Ambrose (pp. 50–51). In terms of content, however, Monreale is clearly to be understood in terms of the Trinity.

❧

The christological interpretation of Gen 18 goes back to the dawn of patristic theology. It has a thoroughly solid basis in the text of Scripture itself—just as the early Church had learnt to read it, that is, in the light of Christ, to whom indeed the whole of Scripture points in a hidden way (Jn 5.39), and in whom it is fulfilled (Matt 1.22ff.). For in Gen 18.1 (LXX), it says that "God" appeared to Abraham at the terebinth of Mambre. In the following verse, it is a matter of "three men," whom Abraham addresses as "my Lord." At the end of the visit, the Lord departs from Abraham (18.33), while only the "two angels" go down to Sodom (19.1).

Clearly, Abraham has taken part in a manifestation of God. The Lord (*kyrios*) visited him in the form of a man, accompanied by two messengers (*angeloi*), who carried out his will. The image of the invisible God (the Father), however, is

5 Cf. Engemann, "Dreifaltigkeitsdarstellungen," p. 158.

Christ, according to the understanding of the early Christians (Col 1.15). He is the Lord (Acts 2.36ff.). Accordingly, in reality the theophanies of the Old Testament are without exception christophanies—manifestations of Christ and hidden fore-shadowings of the Incarnation of the Son.

In this sense, St Justin Martyr already takes the Lord to be God the Logos, whom two angels accompany. This interpretation was widespread up to the fourth century.[6] In much the same way, Evagrios, whose whole mysticism is thoroughly Trinitarian, writes in a letter in which he handles Gen 18 in a symbolic-allegorical way:

> We know that you love Christ so much and that nothing is more hon-oured in your eyes that the "knowledge of Christ." Become now like your fellow-citizen, apply yourself to your name, and remain outside your tent, while this world is for you as "shadows." With your virtues nourish yourself on the "calf," in order to be ready for "hospitality." You have indeed a "Sarah" as "helper," who is eager. I know of her, that she serves God with the "unleavened bread of sincerity and truth." May the Lord grant that the "noon day" of your virtue be bright, and your "tent" become a resting-place for the holy angels and for Christ, our Redeemer.[7]

⸎

Around the year 1000, we first formally encounter unmistakable christological depictions of Gen 18, which on account of their titles are, however, to be understood in a Trinitarian way. Previous to that time, none of Abraham's three guests is characterized as a type of Christ by any particular attributes (scroll, cross nimbus, and so forth). We have already interpreted this equality of form in a Trinitarian way. That they can, however, have another, namely a christological, meaning is the lesson of two liturgical texts of St Romanos the Melodist († about 560).

> Once when the faithful Sarah, in her barrenness longed to give
>   birth,
> Before Isaac her son was born,
> She received God himself in human form, with two archangels,
> And the word came to her at that hour,
> "to Sarah a son shall be."[8]

Even in the sixth century, Romanos represents the traditional christological interpretation, for "God in human form" is naturally Christ. The following kontakion, which not only refers to Gen 18, but also gives a theological interpretation, explains how Romanos understood this Old Testament christophany.

> When God was seen by Abraham, sitting at the oak of Mambre,
> He was beheld as man, without Abraham knowing who he was, for
>   he did not announce it;
> To us now it is not so, for, in his own person, the Word became
>   flesh;
> There a puzzle, here clarity;
> For the fathers shadows, for the patriarchs images,

6 Justin, *Dialogue* 56.5; Irenaeus, *Haer* IV.7.4 etc.; Origen, *Hom in Gen* IV.1 and 5; *Const Apost* V.20.5: Eusebios *HE* I.2.7–9; idem, *Theol Eccl* II.21; Athanasius, *Contra Arianos* I.38; Gerontius, *Vita Melaniae* 47. The same interpretation appears again in the sixth century: Barsanouphios, *ep.* 459.

7 Evagrios Pontikos, *ep.* 33.3 (cf. G. Bunge, *Briefe aus dem Wüste*, Trier 1986, p. 247f.). Cf. also n. 3.

8 *Sancti Romani Melodi Cantica Genuina*, ed. P. Maas and C. A. Trypanis, Oxford 1963, 279 (*cant.* 35.8 on the Nativity of the Virgin Mary).

But for the children, the truth itself;
Once God was seen by Abraham, but he did not see God;
But we behold him, because he wills it, and we lay hold on
the One who appears and gives light to all.[9]

"He was beheld as man [according to another reading: as an angel], without Abraham knowing who he was," therefore, without making him conscious that here the later "Word made flesh" was present in hidden form. Abraham looked at three men (or three angels), one of whom was, unbeknown, the Lord. The lack of differentiation between the three visitors can therefore have the sense of hiding the Lord. This is, then, an expression of that puzzle (*ainigma*), which Abraham cannot solve.

Such a christological meaning, in no way excluding a Trinitarian one, is implied by the immediate context of the mosaics of S. Maria Maggiore and S. Vitale. In the (upper) scene of welcome in S. Maria Maggiore, the middle figure is distinguished from the two accompanying figures by a mandorla that completely envelops it. This middle figure clearly symbolizes Christ in the clothing of the youthful Logos.[10] Should not then the lower scene of the entertainment be also understood christologically, or even eucharistically? Characteristically, the preceding mosaic sets forth the presentation of bread and wine, which Melchisedec brought out for the victorious Abraham (Gen 14.18–20). A (bearded) Christ, leaning down from heaven to Melchisedec and blessing him, brings out here the typological relationship of Christ and Melchisedec, well known from the Epistle to the Hebrews.

This message is even clearer in the mosaics of S. Vitale. Here, the entertainment of the three men is united with the sacrifice of Isaac in a single picture. Likewise, the sacrifices of Abel and Melchisedec are united in a single picture on the opposite wall. These mosaics, moreover, decorate the altar space of the church. The S. Vitale mosaics are, therefore, to be understood on a deeper, spiritual (or mystical) level in a christological/eucharistic way. We shall soon see that this in no way excludes a Trinitarian interpretation on the typological level.

&

The fourth century was not only the century of the heresy of Arius, but, in a bitter struggle with this many-headed monster, also the golden age of patristic Trinitarian theology. The fruit of this state of affairs is the henceforth unshakable confession of the consubstantiality of the persons of Father, Son, and Holy Spirit, distinguished as hypostases (persons). This newly achieved clarity soon made its mark, too, on the exegesis of Gen 18, without completely suppressing the traditional, christological interpretation. From the Greek East, (Pseudo?-) Didymos the Blind (†389) provides an interesting passage utilizing this exegesis. After citing several angelic appearances, which he interpreted as the Holy Spirit, Didymos continues:

Then the Son and the Holy Spirit were called "angel" at the oak of Mambre, when the glorious Trinity was seen by Abraham to announce to him things unknown.[11]

9 Ibid., p. 43 (*cant.* 6.4 on the Theophany). A variant in the second line reads, "he was beheld as an angel"! More examples of Old Testament manifestations of God follow in the other verses: Jacob's ladder (6.5), Moses' cleft in the rock (6.6), the throne of Isaias (6.7).

10 Cf. John Chrysostom, *In cap. XVIII Gen., Hom.* 41 (PG 53.380). "Do not be surprised that, even though the guests, whom he receives, are three, yet the righteous one reaches out as to one, saying, Lord! Probably one of the visitors, to whom he addressed his request, appeared more glorious (*philodoxoteros*)." Chrysostom clearly thinks of the Logos as the Lord.

11 Didymos, *De Trinitate* II.8.3 (PG 39.628). The authenticity of this treatise is disputed.

Didymos sees in the three men who visited Abraham a symbol of the Trinity, but in the two angels, types of the Son and the Spirit, who according to the scriptural text accompanied the Lord, that is, the Father. In the first book of his work *De Trinitate*, which is no longer extant, Didymos had clearly treated this is more detail.[12]

We find the same Trinitarian interpretation, too, in St Cyril of Alexandria (†444). Starting from the peculiar fact that God certainly appears to Abraham in the form of three men, and yet speaks of himself in the singular, and is also so addressed by Abraham, the church father sees in this a picture of the togetherness of the three divine persons as preserving the equality of their essence.[13]

From the West comes a particularly beautiful passage from St Ambrose of Milan (†397):

> Yielding to God in faithfulness, eager in service and ready to serve, Abraham sees, in his readiness to receive the guests, the Trinity in figure (*in typo*): while he receives three and worships one, he binds together hospitality and piety (*religio*). And while preserving the distinction of the persons, he nevertheless gave to one of them the name "Lord," to the three offering one glory and indicating one power.
>
> For it was not teaching, but grace, that spoke in him. And he who had not been taught believed better than we who have been. For no one has falsified the picture (*typum*) of the truth. He saw three, and worshipped the unity. He brought out three measures of fine meal, yet sacrificed one calf, believing that one sacrifice, a gift for the three, was sufficient: one sacrifice, the grace of the three.[14]

Here, Ambrose is closely dependent on Origen, without being constrained by him. The great Alexandrine had indeed written:

> This, however, is not hidden from the wise man receiving them. He meets three, and worships one, and he speaks to one, saying, "Turn aside to your servant, and rest yourself under the tree."[15]

While Origen, however, understood this "one" as the Lord, that is, Christ,[16] and the two companions, faithful to the text of Scripture, as two angels, Ambrose understood the whole in a Trinitarian way. The development of doctrine in the Church had not stood still, but had in the fourth century reached its full Trinitarian profundity. No wonder then, that Rufinus (†410/411) not only translates Origen, but also (in a Trinitarian sense) improves him: For him, the three men are three angels in whom he then sees a hidden reference to the *mysterium Trinitatis*.[17]

Later, St Augustine (†430) again takes up the exegesis of his mentor Ambrose almost word for word in his *tres vidit, et unum adoravit*,[18] which he explains in the following manner:

> Since indeed three men are seen, and none of them is said to be greater than the others in either form or age or power, why should we not here

12 Didymos, ibid. II.23 (PG 39.744/745), where he discusses Gen 18 in connection with the Trinity, refers to the "first Logos."

13 Cyril of Alexandria, *Contra Julianum* I (PG 76.532C-533B).

14 Ambrose, *De Excessu fratris sui Satyri* II.96 (PL 16.1342C).

15 Origen, *Hom. Gen.* 4.2 (SC 7bis, p. 148).

16 Ibid. 4.1 and 5.

17 Origen, *Comm. in Cant.* II.8 (SC 375, p. 410).

18 Augustine, *Contra Maxim.* II.26.7 (PL 42.809).

recognize the equality of the Trinity visibly intimated through the visible creature, and one and the same substance in three persons?[19]

As we have seen in Chapter 2, this interpretation is prescribed in the words of the inscriptions for the mosaics in Monreale and Palermo.

Although the Trinitarian interpretation eventually became used more exclusively, the three interpretations continued side by side for quite some time. Procopius of Gaza (†circa 538), the compiler of a catena on the Octateuch (a collection of ancient interpretations of the books of Genesis to Ruth), draws together the multiple possibilities of meaning as follows:

> Regarding the three men [who appeared to Abraham], some maintain that these are three angels; the Judaïzers teach that one of the three was God, while the other two were angels; others again say that these, who were addressed in the singular as the "Lord," are a figure (*typos*) of the Holy and Consubstantial Trinity.[20]

The Trinitarian interpretation is appropriated in the following century by St Maximos the Confessor (†662). Starting from the threefold number of the visitors, whom Abraham yet addresses in the singular as "my Lord," he speaks of the "threefold manifestation" (that is, in three persons) of God and his "single speech" (that is, in the singular) in relation to "Abraham who was perfect in knowledge."[21] This language was again taken up by the theologian and hymnographer Metrophanes of Smyrna (9th century).

As we have demonstrated, the mosaics of S. Maria Maggiore and S. Vitale have on the typological level first of all a Trinitarian meaning, which does not take away from the christological/eucharistic sense suggested by the context in which they are found. Neither excludes the other. For if the Lord, who appeared to Abraham, may also be understood as the Logos in his hidden presence, so can the threefold number of the visitors be equally interpreted as a reference to the threeness of the persons.

It is in this sense, therefore, that the almost perfect equality of form of Abraham's three guests is to be understood. Other elements of the composition, too, can be understood in the same way: for example, the three same-shaped loaves on the table and the one—not yet divided—sacrificial animal on a plate that Abraham offers his guests. The threefold repetition of a symbol or a letter is, as we have seen, a favourite means of indicating the *mysterium Trinitatis*. Later icon painters depict three chalices instead of three loaves. If one attends to these details, one can hardly avoid the impression that the artists wanted to translate the above-cited meditation by St Ambrose on the oneness and threeness of God into pictorial form.

The mosaics of the fifth and sixth centuries have their direct (extant) successors in the Greco-Norman mosaics of the twelfth century. Yet there are already partial signs of the influence of a new iconographic type that, in the meantime, had developed in the Byzantine East.

☙

19 Augustine, *De Trinitate* II.11.20 (PL 42.858).

20 Procopius, *In Gen. 18* (PG 87.364AB).

21 Maximos the Confessor, *Quaestiones ad Thalassium* 28.lines 10–15, 78–80 (ed. C. Laga and C. Steel, Corpus Christianorum Series Graeca 7, Turnhout 1980, pp. 203, 207).

The last great heresy that shook the Greek East to its roots for more than a century (730–843) was *Iconoclasm*, which, at an intellectual level, called into question the traditional veneration of icons and, at a practical level, systematically destroyed all accessible holy pictures. Through great tribulations and with a truly distinguished sureness of touch from the very beginning, Orthodox theology found itself compelled to justify the ancient practice of the veneration of holy pictures and direct it within Orthodox parameters.[22] Evidently, this period of destruction and new beginnings had its impact on iconography.

As we have seen, it is at the turn of the millennium that we first encounter a new type in the depiction of the *Philoxenia* (Hospitality) of Abraham. Formally, it is certainly christological, yet the use of the title "The Holy Trinity" indicates that it is to be "read" in a Trinitarian manner. How is this apparent contradiction to be explained? Let us begin with the formal, purely iconographic aspect.

Among the patristic witnesses that St John of Damascus (†circa 750) gathered together in his third treatise in the defence of the holy icons, there is the following passage from Eusebios of Caesarea (†339). After the church historian has set out the usual christological interpretation of Gen 18, he continues:

> Thus even to this day the place [of the manifestation] is held to be divine and venerated by those who live nearby in honour of those who appeared to Abraham, and the terebinth remains to be seen and also, in a picture, those who were welcomed by Abraham, reclining, one on each side, and in the middle one better and greater in honour. The one who thus appears signifies to us the Lord himself, our Saviour, whom those men reverence in ignorance of who he is, persuaded by his divine words. Hidden in human form and shape, he showed to our God-loving forefather, Abraham, who he was, and delivered to him knowledge of the Father, and from that he planted seed of piety among human kind.[23]

We have already seen what this picture (*graphē*) originally meant.[24] With the reformulation of the iconographic canon after the final victory of the venerators of the icons in the ninth and tenth centuries, this witness, now robbed of its context, must have seemed to be an exact description of a depiction of the hospitality of Abraham, already highly venerated in the Constantinian period (or even earlier). This supposed archetype must have long ceased to exist,[25] yet it was a simple matter to complete a copy on the basis of Eusebios', or John Damascene's, description. What was important above all was that the central figure, distinguished as the Lord and therefore Christ, was made conspicuous. This is the case with the formally purely christological depictions first attested to around the year 1000. That these supposed archetypes, not otherwise directly attested, originated in Mambre, is evident from a comparison with the pilgrim souvenirs mentioned in chapter 2 (plate 1).[26]

❧

As we have seen, an angelological interpretation of the scene of Gen 18 is of long standing, and pictorial depictions of the scene were from the beginning formally angelological and long remained so. For the depiction of all three of Abraham's

22 See C. von Schönborn, *L'Icône du Christ: Fondements théologiques élaborés entre le Ier et le IIe Concile de Nicée (325–787)*, Paradosis 24, Fribourg en Suisse: Éditions Universitaires 1976.

23 Eusebios, *Demonstratio Evangelica* V.9.7–8 (GCS Eusebios 6, Berlin 1913, p. 232): quoted in John Damascene, *On the Divine Images* III.67 (Eng. trans., Crestwood, NY: St Vladimir's Seminary Press, 2003, p. 121).

24 See the Excursus.

25 Eusebios, *Vita Constantini* III.52, followed by Sozomen, *Historia Ecclesiastica* II.4, expressly says that Constantine had caused the "idols" found at Mambre to be burned by fire. The "picture" mentioned can hardly have escaped this destruction, even if Eusebios in his *Dem. Ev.* does not designate it as an idol.

26 Eusebios seems to indicate that the central figure was in some way distinguished from the others and so could be described as "better and greater in honour." On the pilgrim souvenir, the three angels are of equal size. More importantly, two essential elements of the seal are missing from the Christian witnesses from the tenth century onwards, namely, the birdcage and the fountain and the gestures of the angels, corresponding to these. See also the Excursus.

visitors as angels was retained in the formally properly christological depictions of the second type and given even clearer expression: All three figures, including the middle one, now have wings and carry messenger staves in their hands. Even when the middle figure is designated by other attributes as Christ, such a depiction as an angel was thoroughly plausible, for Christ bears the honorary title of "Angel of Great Counsel" (Is 9:6), which, if rare in the Old Testament, is well known from the liturgical office (Great Compline).[27]

In contradiction to this formally christological interpretation, there stands the now recurring title of this type—"The Holy Trinity"—which henceforth makes clear that, with the triumph of the venerators of the icons in the ninth century and the reshaping of Orthodox iconography, the Trinitarian interpretation of Gen 18 is firmly established.

The theologian and prolific hymnographer St Metrophanes of Smyrna (ninth century), in his famous canons on the Trinity that would have been most familiar to the devout monk Andrei Rublev from the midnight office, often speaks of the visit of God to Abraham.

> Of old you were clearly seen by Abraham, triple in hypostasis but one in the nature of the Godhead, the purest teaching of the Godhead made known in figures; faithfully we hymn you, God, sole ruler and triple-sunned.[28]

> While still an exile, Abraham was counted worthy, to receive in figural form, you, the unique Lord, in three hypostases, beyond being, in human forms.[29]

Here, as in the four other texts in which he interprets Gen 18, Metrophanes points out—as Romanos the Melodist had already done—that the manifestation of God "in human dress" was a symbol. It was not the personal identity of Father, Son, and Spirit that was revealed to Abraham, but rather the unity of essence, and the threeness of the persons of the Holy Trinity. Just as Romanos before him, Metrophanes sees that the Old Testament contains only "holy signs," the reality of which is first revealed in the New Covenant. Yet this truth is no longer for him, as it was for Romanos, the mysterious presence of God the Logos in the company of two angels, but the Holy Trinity itself.

☙

It is easy to recognize that the Trinitarian vision would not in the long run be satisfied with the christological iconographic type and its straightforward identification of the Son. Over the centuries, the iconographers responded to the need for a greater harmony between picture and title in various ways. The transfer of the attributes, which originally characterized the central angel alone, to the other angels was not quite adequate (cf. plate 12). The solution lay in the complete renunciation of these attributes.

In the late Byzantine period, a third iconographic type developed, which in its pure form portrayed the three angels as identical (cf. plate 14). Interestingly, this had also been the case with the first type. Around 1500, the painter of a Russian icon went so far as to make even the gestures and the posture of the three

27 The text of Didymos the Blind, cited on pp. 49–50, may be recalled, where the two angels, accompanying the Lord, are designated as Son and Spirit. It is perhaps a matter of a—indeed quite singular—*ad hoc* exegesis, created by the need to detect Old Testament *testimonia* for the consubstantial persons of the Holy Trinity.

28 *Paraklitiki*, Sunday, Canon for the Midnight Office, tone 1, ode 3, troparion 1.

29 Ibid., tone 3, ode 6, troparion 1.

angels completely identical and to return to the frontal view of the early mosaics (plate 18).

Especially clear in this development is the trouble taken to make manifest the unity of essence in the threeness of the hypostases. In this connexion, there was a conscious renunciation of any attempt to make visible the attributes of the persons. The question of which angel symbolizes Father, Son, and Spirit is meaningless. Nothing allows one to read from this Trinitarian type anything about the intra-Trinitarian relationships of the three divine persons. The icons achieve an abstract character, comparable in a way to the geometrical figures used as symbols of the Trinitarian God that were coming into fashion in the West.

❧

The changes in the interpretation of Gen 18 and their iconographical impact, indicated here in broad outline, can be regarded in retrospect as a continual deepening of the central mystery of the Christian faith. This change had a beautiful impact on the depiction of the two human figures, Abraham and Sarah, who are inseparably bound up with this picture. Their depiction reflects the changing attitude of the faithful to the *mysterium Trinitatis*, whether intended or not. If we look back over the development in the depiction of the Hospitality of Abraham from the fresco in the catacomb on the Via Latina, then we can trace the following steps.

The primary content of the Old Testament account of the visit of the three men to Abraham is the promise of the birth of Isaac, who, in the Christian-typological understanding, is a prefiguration of Christ. Accordingly, neither Abraham nor Sarah is a simple bystander. The mosaics of the fifth to the thirteenth centuries therefore always depict Sarah, laughing and, at times, doubting, at the entrance to the tent. There is scarcely any indication that the Lord, accompanied by the two angels, is, in Christian understanding, "Our Lord Jesus Christ." In Romanos' interpretation, Abraham does not know whom it is he has welcomed.

With the appearance of an also formally straightforward christological type about the year 1000 that includes a Trinitarian inscription, the placing of Abraham and Sarah in the whole composition begins to change. Finally, they stand together serving before the angelic figures symbolizing the Holy Trinity. In the third, late Byzantine type, which is distinguished among other things by its broad layout, they are often inserted between the figures. The simple entertainment of the three mysterious guests has become an act of reverent worship of the Holy Trinity.

This feature also casts a light on another aspect of several icons of this type. The architectural background changes from the biblical items of house, tree, and, eventually, rock into a scene of a timeless realm. The worship of the three divine guests takes place not at the biblical Mambre, but somewhere that could even be a church. It is, therefore, drawn into the present: Here and now Abraham and Sarah worship the All-holy Trinity.

It is interesting, moreover, to observe that the chalice in the middle of the table, in which can be seen the head of the calf that Abraham has set before his guests, acquires great significance in the third, late Byzantine type. The central angel, who even now is often designated as Christ, no longer raises his hand in blessing but, looking directly at the beholder, points to this vessel. Here, the emphasis has been moved from the promise of the birth of Isaac to his sacrifice:

the Old Testament type of Christ's sacrifice on the Cross, that on his part is present in the unbloody sacrifice of the Divine Liturgy.

Since Gen 18 will, from the ninth century onwards, be ordinarily understood as a manifestation of the Holy Trinity, the Old Testament event is therefore only an image and holy sign of the New Testament truth, and Abraham and Sarah are now fundamentally simply bystanders, who can be dropped if need be. This happened from time to time long before Rublev.

PLATE 18

Russian icon from Pskov, Tretiakov Gallery, Moscow; fifteenth/ sixteenth century.

55

The earliest example known to us of this final reduction to the bare essentials is found in a double portrait of the Byzantine emperor John VI Kantakouzenos, from between 1347 and 1354 (Plate 19). Here, the emperor as monk holds in his left hand a scroll with the words "Great is the God of the Christians"—which means naturally: the Holy Trinity—while his right hand points up to a depiction of the three angels. Not only are the angels depicted without Abraham and Sarah, but they appear without any kind of biblical context. Only the table and the vessels placed on it, especially the middle one, with the calf's head, call it to mind.

With this, the long and gradual process by which the depiction of Abraham's three visitors became independent of its biblical context reaches its climax. These figures now represent the most perfect type of that most profound of Christian mysteries, the *mysterium Trinitatis*. Rublev will again, under the powerful influence of older models, introduce this biblical context in the form of house, tree, and rock, yet he will also renounce Abraham and Sarah, in contrast to the immediate predecessors of his own *Troitsa*. They have become superfluous, as on the above-mentioned miniature. The worshippers of the All-holy Trinity are now all those who behold its holy icon with faith.

PLATE 19

Double portrait of Emperor John VI Kantakouzenos (1347–1354),
Paris, Bibliothèque Nationale; fourteenth century.

CHAPTER FOUR

Sergii of Radonezh

This complex theological and iconographic prehistory was, of course, neither known to Andrei Rublev, nor consciously present to him, although it determined his work, even in details. What was present to him was the unique figure of St Sergii of Radonezh (1314–92), under whose luminous influence he painted his *Troitsa*. Without some knowledge of this great father of monks, Rublev's *Trinity* cannot be understood. What interests us here is less the historical-political role of Sergii, which is closely bound up with the emergence of the Muscovite state, than his spiritual image, as it is set before us by his disciples and followers.

❧

Soon after the death of Sergii of Radonezh, who was already venerated as a saint in his own lifetime, Epifanii the Wise composed a biography that was something more than an edifying legend. In the prologue to his *Life*, he gives the following account of his work.

> Many a thing that I heard and understood my fathers narrated to me, many a thing I heard from the old men, and many a thing I saw with my eyes, and many a thing I heard from his mouth; and many a thing I learned from those who for not a little time followed him and poured water on his hands, and many a thing I also heard from his older brother Stefan, who according to the flesh was the father of Fedor, the Archbishop of Rostov. The other things I heard from the other elders, ancient and trustworthy, who were eyewitnesses to his life, his education and learning, his childhood and his taking of the monastic vow. Still other elders were truthful eyewitnesses and observers of his taking of the monastic vow and of the beginning of his eremitic life and of his appointment to the office of hegumen.
>
> I am perplexed that so many years have passed and yet the story of his life is still not written. And this I regret much because already twenty and six years have elapsed since this Holy *Starets*, most wonderful and most kind, passed away, and nobody has dared to write about him; neither one from afar nor one who is near; neither one who is great nor one who is small, those who are great because they did not wish to, those who are small because they did not dare to. One or two years after the *Starets* had passed away, I, cursed and impudent, having sighed to God and having called in my prayer upon the *Starets*, dared this and I began writing. I detailed, little by little, the life of the *Starets*. I said to myself in secret: I am not stealing a path from anyone but I am writing for myself for the sake of preservation and memory and benefit.[1]

1 M. Klimenko, *The "Vita" of St Sergii of Radonizh*, pp. 68f., 67 (A. A. Hackel, *Sergii of Radonezh*, pp. 48f.)

Epifanii proceeded so scrupulously that we may assume that his *Life of St Sergii* at all events reflects that picture that the saint left in the memory of his chosen witnesses.

Like many much-read texts, the *Life of St Sergii* was soon reworked and supplemented.[2] One of these reworkings comes from Pachomii Logofet, a Serbian monk, who lived in Moscow about 1450, and to whom we owe also a *Life* of the first disciple of Sergii, St Nikon of Radonezh. It is this later and reworked redaction that we use as the basis for this chapter for the following reasons.

If one compares Epifanii's original version with Pachomii's reworked version, then it is striking that the whole unique relationship that Sergii had to the mystery of the Holy Trinity, already clearly set forth by Epifanii, was developed by Pachomii into a *leitmotiv*, which runs like a scarlet thread through the whole of the saint's life. The question whether Pachomii the Serb had based this on historically reliable sources is only of interest to the historian. For it is striking that this Trinitarian emphasis is absent from the *Life of Nikon* that came from his own pen. All that is important for us is that Pachomii clearly reproduced the picture of the saint that had been handed down from the saintly founder at the Trinity Monastery in the generation after Sergii and towards the end of Nikon's time; that is, precisely at the time when Andrei Rublev was working there. It is a reflection, therefore, of the spiritual climate in which Rublev beheld and painted his *Troitsa*.

❧

The particular vocation of the future saint was proclaimed already before his birth. When his pious mother attended the Divine Liturgy one Sunday as usual, the child in her womb suddenly made his voice heard three times: at the reading of the Gospel, at the beginning of the so-called Cherubic Hymn when the priest took the gifts to the altar, and, a third time, when the celebrant invited the faithful to communion with the exclamation: "The Holy Things for the Holy!" The meaning of this incredible event only became clear at the baptism of the child.[3]

> After six weeks, on the fortieth day after his birth, his parents brought the child into God's church, presenting him according to tradition and as they had promised to present him to God, who had given him. Likewise they asked the priest to perform Holy Baptism. The priest elevated him, prayed over him and baptized him with spiritual joy and carefulness in the name of the Father, the Son and the Holy Spirit. In Holy Baptism he gave him the name Varfolomei. Having richly received the grace of the Holy Spirit, he lifted him from the font of baptismal water and perceived by the Divine Spirit that the child would be a "chosen vessel" (Acts 9:15).
>
> But his father and his mother, having not a poor knowledge of Holy Scripture, told the priest how the child had cried three times in church when he was still being carried in his mother's womb: "What it will signify, we do not know." But the priest, whose name was Mikhail and who was versed in books, explained to them from Holy Scripture, from both Testaments, the Old and the New, and said: "David said in the Psalms: 'Thy eyes beheld my unformed substance' (Ps 138.16). And the Lord himself by His holy mouth said to His disciples: 'You have been with me from

2 For the sources, cf. Müller, *Dreifaltigkeitsikone.*

3 Klimenko, "*Vita,*" pp. 73f. (Hackel, p. 50).

the beginning' (Jn 15.27). In the Old Testament the prophet Jeremiah was consecrated in his mother's womb (Jer 1.5). In the New Testament the Apostle Paul has proclaimed: 'God, the Father of our Lord Jesus Christ, set me apart when I was in my mother's womb to reveal His Son in me, that I might preach about Him among the heathen' (Gal 1.15–16)." And he told them many other things from Holy Scripture. About the child he told the parents: "Do not mourn over this, but rather rejoice and be glad, for he will be a vessel chosen by God, an abode of and a servant to the Holy Trinity." And so it was. And so he blessed the child and his parents and dismissed them to their home.[4]

❧

What was meant by this vocation to be "God's chosen vessel" and the "abode and servant of the Holy Trinity" will be revealed by a wonderful encounter, which must have deeply marked the "child consecrated in his mother's womb."

One day his father sent him to seek the foals. All this happened by the providence of the most wise God, as the Book of Kings also informs us about Saul, who was sent by his father Kish to seek the lost donkey. But Saul went and found the holy prophet Samuel who anointed him to the Kingdom. And thus Saul rose to higher works than assigned. And in a like manner, this blessed lad also rose to work higher than his assignment. He was sent by his father Kiril to seek the lost cattle and he met a strange and unknown monk, a holy *starets* with the rank of a presbyter. He was of beautiful and of angelic appearance and stood in the field under an oak tree praying in tears most fervently. The lad saw him, bowed humbly before him to the earth, approached him and stood near him, waiting for the end of his prayer. And when the *starets* finished and looked at the lad, he recognized with his inward eyes that he would be a vessel chosen by the Holy Spirit. He invited him and called him to draw nearer. He blessed him and gave him a kiss of Christ and, asking, he said: "What are you seeking, or what do you want, child?" The lad answered: "My soul loves and desires—more than anything— to acquire learning. I was given the chance to learn but now my soul is grieving much, for I try to learn and I cannot. So you, holy father, pray to God for me that I may be able to acquire learning."

The *starets* lifted his hands and eyes to heaven and, sighing to God, he prayed fervently. After the prayer he said, "Amen!" And he took something from his pocket as if it were a treasure and with his three fingers he handed it to him. It looked like prosphora, a little piece of white wheaten bread from Holy Communion. And he said to him: "Open your mouth, child, take it and eat it. It is given to you as a sign of God's grace and of understanding of the Holy Scriptures. Although it seems to be small, great is the sweetness of its eating." The lad opened his mouth and ate it. And he felt its sweetness in his mouth as if from sweet honey, and he said, "Is it not of this that it was written, 'How sweet are Thy words to my palate! Sweeter than honey to my mouth' (Ps 118.103), and 'My soul loves

4 Klimenko,"*Vita*," pp. 76f. (Hackel, p. 53f.)

61

them very much' (Ps 118.167)." And the *starets* said to him: "If you believe, you shall see greater things. And about learning, do not worry, child. May it be known to you that from this day on the Lord will grant you a very good understanding of learning, more than your brothers and school-mates." And he instructed him for the benefit of his soul.[5]

When the anxious mother asked the holy *starets* afresh about the strange sign of the threefold crying from her womb, the parents received the following answer:

"O blessed virtue! O, most kind matrimony, being parents to such a child! Why are you afraid from fear when there is no fear? Rather, rejoice and be merry that you were found worthy of giving birth to such a child, whom God marked while still in his mother's womb. Now, I will say one last word and then I will desist from my speech. This will be a sign to you that my words will be fulfilled. After my departure you will see that the lad will know all learning and will understand all the holy books. And the second sign to you, an annunciation, is that this lad, because of his virtu-ous life, will be great before God and men."

The *starets* said this and departed (after having prophesied in obscure words to them that their son would be a dwelling place of the Holy Trinity and that he would make many people follow him in the understanding of the Divine commandments). And after he had said this, he left them. They accompanied him until they were before the house gate. But he suddenly became invisible. They were perplexed and thought that he was an angel sent to grant their lad knowledge of learn-ing . . . Upon the departure of the *starets* it was found that the lad sud-denly understood all learning well. He had changed in a strange manner and whatever book he opened, he read well and understood it . . . He obeyed his parents in everything, striving to follow all their instructions and in nothing to disobey them, as the Scripture also says: "Honour thy father and mother, that thy days may be long in the land (Ex 20.12)."[6]

❧

Thenceforth, the youth led a strictly ascetic life, although he still lived in the world, "and so the grace of the Holy Spirit took possession of him."[7] When still very young, Varfolomei became a hermit, together with his brother Stefan, who meanwhile had been widowed and become a monk. After they had built in the wilderness their cells and a small wooden church, the following dialogue took place between the brothers:

The blessed lad said to Stefan: "Since you are my older brother in the fam-ily, according to the flesh, but even more so according to the spirit, it seems that I should have you in place of a father. And now I have no one except you to ask about everything. I beseech you and ask you most of all about this: this church is now erected and completed and it is time to consecrate it. Tell me, in which name should we consecrate this church and the name of which saint should we celebrate?" Stefan answered:

5 Klimenko, "*Vita*," pp. 84f. (Hackel, pp. 56f.).

6 Klimenko, "*Vita*," pp. 87f. (Hackel, pp. 59f.).

7 Ibid., p. 88.

"Why do you ask me and why to you tempt and torture me? You yourself know better than I? . . . God elected you when you still were carried in your mother's womb . . . to teach many others to believe in the Holy Trinity. Thus it is more fitting than anything else that you consecrate this church in the name of the Holy Trinity. It is not our own wish, but God's will and manifestation and providence. God wanted it so. The Lord's name be blessed forever."

And when Stefan had said this, the blessed lad sighed from his heart and said: "You have spoken the truth, my Lord. This is agreeable to me, too. . . . My soul wishes to do this and consecrate the church to the name of the Holy Trinity, but for the sake of humility I asked you, and now the Lord my God did not forsake me, and gave me the wish of my own heart."[8]

❧

Some time later, Stefan, discouraged by the severity of this life in the wilderness, left his brother and entered a monastery in Moscow. Varfolomei, still a layman, remained alone in the wilderness. Finally, he received monastic consecration from an otherwise unknown starets, Igumen Mitrofan, who

> tonsured him into the angelic state in the month of October, on the seventh day, on the memorial day of the holy martyrs, Sergii and Bacchos [1342]. And in the monastic rank he was named Sergii. . . . The saint was twenty-three years old at the time when he assumed the monastic order. The church which was erected by Sergii himself, and which he consecrated in the name of the Holy Trinity, this church now served him. After the tonsuring in this church, the afore-named hegumen celebrated the Divine Liturgy. The blessed Sergii, the newly consecrated monk, as he was thus made perfect, became a participant in the Communion of the Holy Sacrament and he thus shared the body and blood of our Lord Jesus Christ. As a worthy one he was found worthy of receiving such a Holy Sacrament. And thus the grace and gift of the Holy Spirit entered him after Holy Communion, or even during the Communion, and dwelt with him. How is this known? There happened to be a few people at that time who became true and unfalse witnesses. When Sergii accepted the Holy Sacrament, the whole church suddenly was filled with fragrance, and not only in the church but the sweet fragrance was smelled even around the church.
>
> This was the first monk who was tonsured in this church and in this wilderness: the first in beginning, the last in worldly wisdom; the first according to number and the last in finishing his work. . . . When he was tonsured, he had not only the hair of his head shaved but, together with the removal of his bodily hair, his carnal desires were taken away. And as he put off his lay clothing, he put aside also his old self, and putting the old self aside, he put on the new man, and firmly girded his loins and prepared himself for spiritual deeds. He left the world and renounced it and all that is in the world; all possessions and all other secular things. With

8 Klimenko, "*Vita*," pp. 96f. (Hackel, p. 66).

one simple word he broke the chains of worldly living. As an eagle who covers himself with his light wings and soars high in the air, so in a like manner the Venerable left the world and all who are in the world.

With this prayer of intercession, the abbot left him to his life, dedicated to God:

Lord God, who has already chose you, he will now make you generous and understanding. He will teach you and fill you with all the spiritual joys.[9]

❧

So, the young monk began his life of renunciation as a hermit under the protection of the grace that he had received at his holy baptism and that had first been revealed outwardly at his monastic consecration, that "second baptism" in the penitential bath of tears.

What kind of a spirit, or which language, can understand or narrate his desires and his early ardour and love of God and the hidden achievements of his virtues? It is also impossible to determine his solitude, his boldness, his groaning, his unceasing praying which was constantly brought before God, his warm tears, the lamentation of his soul, his tender sighing, his all-night vigils, his assiduous singing, his unceasing prayers, his constant standing, his diligent reading, his frequent genuflections, his fasting, thirsting, his lying on the earth, his spiritual poverty and privation of everything. . . . In addition to all this, there were the devilish assaults, visible and invisible fights, struggles, plottings, demonic horrors, diabolic dreams, the horrors of the wilderness, the expectations of the unexpected, troubles, inroads of beasts and their wild attacks. . . . Many beasts used to come to him not only at night but even during the day. There were bestial packs of wolves howling and roaring and sometimes also bears. The Venerable Sergii, as a man, though fearing a little but fervently sending his prayers to God, thus armed himself and hence through the grace of God he remained without harm from them. The beasts withdrew and did not inflict him with a single harm. When he at first began arranging this place, the Venerable Sergii had suffered much animosity and sorrows from demons, from beasts and from reptiles, but none of them had ever touched him, or harmed him, because God's grace guarded him. . . .
And so, Sergii, in the name of the Holy Trinity, having the Holy Mother of God as his helper and protector, and having, instead of a weapon, the honorable Cross of Christ, defeated the devil, as David defeated Goliath. At once the devil with his demons became invisible and all vanished and no one knew where they were. The Venerable Sergii gave many thanks to God, who had delivered him from such devilish tricks.[10]

❧

9 Klimenko, "Vita," pp. 100–03. (Hackel, pp. 69f.).

10 Klimenko, "Vita," pp. 104–06. (Hackel, pp. 71ff.).

Nevertheless the holy *starets* had promised the little Varfolomei not only that he would himself "be one day the dwelling-place of the Holy Trinity," but also that he would "lead many to an understanding of the divine commandments." After he had tasted "the divine sweetness of silence" in deep solitude for two or three years, the first disciples gathered around the young ascetic, and the hermit cell soon became a hermit colony. The brothers urgently asked Sergii to become their abbot, arguing thus:

> Before we came to this place, we heard of your initiation of good deeds and of the church's foundation which you have completed by your own hands, which has the grace of the Holy Trinity, to which we come now and in which we place our hope and expectation under your leadership. So, from now on, be to us our father and hegumen, representing us before the Throne of the Holy Trinity, sending to God the threefold holy song of the Seraphim and performing the bloodless sacrifice and with your hands distribute to us the most Holy Body and Divine Blood of our Lord Jesus Christ. Calm us in our old age and then commit us to the grave.[11]

At first, Sergii refused point-blank, but the brothers persisted just as stubbornly with their demand and even threatened otherwise to leave the community. Finally, a word from the bishop Afanassii settled the matter.

> "My beloved! God said by His Holy Spirit through David's mouth: 'I have exalted one chosen out of the people' and again: 'With whom my hand shall be established, mine arm also shall strengthen him' (Ps 88.20, 22). And the Apostle Paul said: 'No one should take this honour, nor rank, but only he who is called by God' (Heb 5.4). But since you, my son and brother, were called by God from your mother's womb, which I have heard from many people about you, so henceforth you shall be Father and hegumen to the brethren whom God gathered into the shelter of the Holy Trinity." . . .
>
> When the Venerable Father, our Hegumen Sergii, came into his monastery, into the abode of the Holy Trinity, the brethren met him and bowed before him to the earth and were filled with joy. But he entered the church, fell on his face upon the ground, and in tears he performed a prayer to the King Invisible, looking upon the icon of the Holy Trinity and calling upon the Holy Virgin Mary, the Mother of God for help. He called also upon other servants at the Throne of His Heavenly Powers: John the Forerunner and the wise Apostles. And together with them he called upon the original Bishops, Basil the Great, Gregory the Theologian, and John Chrysostom and all the Saints, whose prayers he asked before the right hand of the Pantokrator, that He give him the firm courage to stand at the Throne of the glory of the Life-giving Trinity and to touch by his hands the Lamb of God, Christ the Son of God, who gave Himself as a Sacrifice for the world.[12]

It was less through learned words, than through his holy life, that Sergii became such a model for his brothers.

11 Klimenko, "*Vita*," p. 119 (Hackel, p. 84).

12 Klimenko, "*Vita*," pp. 121–24. (Hackel, pp. 87ff.).

The community remained at first small and poor. A miraculous vision taught Sergii, however, that it was destined to have a great future.

> One day the saint, according to his usual custom, was keepings vigils and was praying for the brethren that the Lord help them in their daily work and improvement. And while he was so praying deep in the night, he heard a voice saying: "Sergii!" But he was very surprised by this unusual night call and, after he said his prayer, he opened the window of his cell, wishing to see who called, and right away he saw a wonderful vision: a great light appeared from heaven and drove away all darkness of the night, and the night was illuminated by this light which excelled by its brightness the light of day. For a second time the voice was heard, saying: "Sergii! You are praying for your children, and the Lord has accepted your praying; look carefully and see a multitude of monks who have gathered in the name of the Holy and Life-giving Trinity in your flock to be taught by you." The saint looked and saw a multitude of very beautiful birds who flew not only over the monastery, but also around the monastery, and the voice was heard, saying: "As you saw these birds, in a like manner the flock of your disciples will be multiplied and even after you they will not diminish if they choose to follow in your footsteps."[13]

The unorganised community of hermits soon developed into a great monastery *(lavra)* under a common rule, which became the spiritual centre of the Principality of Moscow. Indeed, the Trinity Monastery became, even in the lifetime of the founder, the motherhouse of no fewer than eight daughter houses, not counting numerous new foundations by direct disciples or friends of the saint.

All this is without doubt the work of that Holy Spirit, whose chosen vessel Sergii was and who had meanwhile made Sergii's presence known outside by miraculous ways. He had done this first at the monastic consecration of Sergii. The *Life of St Sergii* records, too, another astonishing sign, for which there were also witnesses.

> Some time after that, when the saint was celebrating the Divine Liturgy, there was also present a disciple of the Venerable, ecclesiarch Simon . . . who was perfect in many virtues, of whom also the Holy *Starets* himself witnessed that he had a perfect life. This Simon saw a wonderful vision. Once when the saint was officiating, he said to him that he saw a fire moving over the Table of Oblation, illuminating the altar and encircling the Holy Gifts. And when the saint was about to partake of Holy Communion the divine fire rolled itself up like a shroud and entered the holy chalice. And so the saint took Communion. As Simon saw that, he was frightened, and was filled with trembling and so he marvelled in himself. When the saint moved away from the Table of Oblation, he understood that Simon was granted to see the wonderful vision, and so he called him and said: "Child, why is your spirit frightened?" He said: "My Lord! I saw a wonderful vision that the Grace of the Holy Spirit is operating in you."

13 Klimenko, "*Vita*," p. 151 (Hackel, p. 116).

The saint forbade him and said: "Do not announce to anybody what you saw until the Lord orders my departure from this life." And they rendered praise to the Lord together.[14]

❧

What had been prophesied of Sergii before his birth while in his mother's womb and had manifested time and again in his life was to be fulfilled after his death. The *Life* closes with these striking words:

> Although the saint did not want glory, neither when he was alive nor after his death, the mighty power of God glorified him. At his departure the angels preceded him to heaven, opening before him the doors of paradise and leading him into the longed for blessing, into the refuge of the righteous, into the light of the angels. And what he had always wished he saw: he received the illumination of the Most Holy Trinity (as it befits one who fasts), the adoration of monks.[15]

❧

The meaning of a historical figure, and his message, can be understood both from the impression that he made on his immediate contemporaries and also from the continuing effect exercised beyond his own lifetime. From the deep impression made on the initial biographers of St Sergii of Radonezh and on their many followers who embellished these accounts, as well as from the unique role played by the *mysterium Trinitatis* as the continuing activity of the Holy Spirit in these accounts, one may conclude that a powerful sense of the Spirit and the Holy Trinity radiated from the saint, which neither his immediate disciples nor his spiritual followers could escape.

This truly spiritual Trinitarian mysticism found its most timeless expression in the *Troitsa* of the holy painter-monk Andrei Rublev.

14 Klimenko, "*Vita*," pp. 179f. (Hackel, pp. 145f.).

15 Klimenko, "*Vita*," p. 182 (Hackel, pp. 148f.).

CHAPTER FIVE

Nikon of Radonezh and Andrei Rublev

Unfortunately, no such chronicle as we have for St Sergii of Radonezh exists for St Andrei Rublev. In his case, we are dependent on information that is scarce and scattered.[1] The medieval chroniclers who mention Rublev were concerned almost exclusively with his activity as a painter and knew nothing of his personal life. Even the dates of his life can only be determined approximately.

We can glean some information from the *Life of St Nikon of Radonezh*, written by the same Serbian monk, Pachomii Logofet, who composed St Sergii's *Life*. According to the short version of Nikon's *Life*, Andrei Rublev seems to have died shortly after the completion of the decoration of the stone Church of the Holy Trinity in the Monastery of St Sergii, built by Nikon in 1422, and before the death of the latter (November 17, 1427) in the Andronikov Monastery in Moscow, the community to which he belonged. The compilers of various monastic chronicles first mention Rublev in the year 1405 as a still-young icon painter close to the more famous Feofan Grek, in connexion with the decoration of the Church of the Annunciation in the Moscow Kremlin. In the year 1408, Rublev appears in the company of his friend and "fellow-faster" Daniil, with whom he was to be linked all his life, at the decoration of the Church of the Mother of God in Vladimir.

The conditions under which Andrei and Daniil lived in the St Sergii Monastery are related in the *Life of Nikon*.[2] The great victory of St Dimitrii Donskoi in 1380 had not prevented Tatars, who had ruled Russia since 1237, from returning to the country periodically to exact tribute and to plunder. In 1408, Edigei came right up to the region of present-day Moscow and burnt down the St Sergii Monastery. Nikon had foreseen this devastation in a vision and taken appropriate precautions; he fled with his brothers to a safer place shortly before the arrival of the Tatars.

At the news of this catastrophe, the holy metropolitans of Moscow, Peter and Alexii, who had personally warned Nikon, made a firm promise: The St Sergii Monastery would be rebuilt on a larger scale and more splendidly and in the future would be free from devastation. On his return, Nikon immediately went about the rebuilding of the monastery. Nothing, not even the first Church of St Sergii, which had been built in wood, had withstood the flames. All that the monks could save with any certainty were their personal memories of the saint, which are preserved to this day in the St Sergii Monastery. The two icons that Sergii had in his cell—one of the Mother of God and the other of St Nicholas—were also found.[3]

1 Cf., above all, Mainka, *Rublev's Dreifaltigkeit-sikone* (1986) and Müller, *Dreifaltigkeitsikone*, as well as the presumably later account in Sergejew, *Das heilige Handwerk*.

2 Our account in based on the *Vita* of Nikon, ed. Yablonskij, pp. lxxivff.

3 Cf. the Jubilee volume, *Troitsa-Sergejeva-Lavra*.

First of all, Nikon built a new church (1411), wooden like its predecessor and also dedicated to the Holy Trinity. Soon after, Nikon had a stone church built in its stead (1422). However, the little wooden church was not destroyed but dismantled and reconstructed east of the new church together with its iconostasis. In 1476–77, a stone church was built in place of the wooden church; this was at first also called the Church of the Trinity, and only in the second half of the sixteenth century was its name changed to the Church of the Holy Spirit. Andrei Rublev must have known the great icon of the Trinity from the first of Nikon's churches, as we have already seen. It is probably identical with an icon discovered in the monastery in 1920, which is today in the State Museum in Moscow.[4]

After the church, the abbot built the monks' cells and the rest of the buildings of the monastery, which again immediately became a centre of attraction for monks and the faithful alike. Full of love, Nikon received them all, utterly in the spirit of the Sergii, who welcomed everyone, and nourished them with words of spiritual instruction.

The stone church, begun for the growing community of monks in 1422, was built by Nikon "on the grave of his father," that is, of St Sergii. This church, too, was dedicated to the Holy Trinity; Nikon's biographer, Pachomii the Serb, adds, however, that it was also consecrated "in the memory and glory of his father." Nikon provided costly fittings for the church, which still stands today. Despite the resistance of some of the monks, he finally fulfilled his wish to have it painted. To this end, "he gathered together at once icon-painters accomplished in virtue, Daniil by name and his fellow-faster Andrei and others with them." These painters completed not only the frescos in the church, but also the still-surviving iconostasis at the same time.

Opinion is divided as to whether Rublev painted his famous icon of the Trinity then, or whether he had already painted it at some earlier time, in support of which some stylistic observations are adduced. As emerges from the shorter version of the *Life of Nikon*, the work on the St Sergii Monastery was in any case "the last work of their hands," that Daniil and Andrei "left behind as a memorial." After finishing it, the two painter-monks went back to the Andronikov Monastery in Moscow, where the "humble Andrei" soon died, followed a short while later by Daniil. "Both attained a blessed end, having lived virtuous lives and reached a good age."[5]

At the moment of his departure, Daniil had one of those visions that we encounter generally in many holy monks and devout Christians. He beheld "his beloved Andrei," full of love and calling him into that blessedness, which he had already entered. After he had entrusted his vision to those standing round him, he gave his spirit back into the hands of his creator. The brothers who were staying then at the Andronikov Monastery realized that the abbot Nikon had pressed on with the painting of the Church of the Trinity so urgently because he had foreseen in spirit the death of the two painter-monks—and presumably, too, his own death in the year 1427.

4 For the three preceding paragraphs, see the evidence of Smirnowa, *Moskauer Ikonen*, p. 271.

5 The year of Rublev's death is disputed: Müller, *Dreifaltigkeitsikone*, p. 49: 1427; Mainka, *Rublev's Dreifaltigkeitsikone* (1986), p. 29: January 29, 1430 (with reference to the gravestone).

❦

So ends the account of Pachomii the Serb. Thereafter the memory of Andrei Rublev was not to fade. A particularly fine example comes from the pen of St Iosif of Volokalamsk (1440–1515), who drew on the memories of an abbot of the St Sergii Monastery, Spiridon, from the year 1478.

> The holy Andronik was radiant with great virtues, and together with him were his disciples Sava and Aleksandr and those wonderful and greatly renowned icon painters, Daniil and his disciple Andrei and many others, just the same. And they had such virtues and were so eager for fasting and the monastic way of life, and participated so much in divine grace and were so advanced in divine love, that they never had any care for things earthly, but always raised their minds and their thoughts on high to the immaterial and divine light, while their physical eyes were continually raised to pictures of the Lord, and his all-pure Mother and all the Saints, painted with material colours. So, even on the Feast Day of the radiant Resurrection of Christ, they sat on chairs before the divine and all-pure icons and looked continually at them, whence they were filled with divine joy and radiance. And not only on that day did they do so, but also on other days, if they were not occupied with icon painting. For this reason, they were also glorified by their Lord, Christ, in their hour of death. Andrei died first, but afterwards his friend Daniil fell sick, too, and as he gave up the spirit, he saw his friend Andrei in great glory, with great joy calling him into the eternal and unending blessedness.[6]

Regardless of its factual nature, the tradition that grew up around Rublev in monastic circles within fifty years after his death witnesses to the growing regard in which he was held—together with his friend Daniil—in the Russian Church. The possession of icons by Rublev already fed the pride of notables, both spiritual and secular, who were prepared to offer quite large sums to acquire them. Iosif himself possessed three icons from the hand of Rublev; according to an inventory from the year 1545, his monastery is mentioned as possessing nine icons ascribed to Rublev.[7]

If one could not possess an original Rublev icon, there was always the possibility of having a copy made as faithfully as possible. In a testament for the high regard in which Rublev's *Troitsa* enjoyed already in the fifteenth century, the monk Paisii (1484–85), perhaps at Iosif's wish, painted such a copy for the Monastery Cathedral dedicated to the Dormition of the Mother of God (plate 20). It is somewhat larger (151 x 120 cm) than the original (142 x 112 cm). Paisii also allowed himself some freedom, always granted to an icon painter, in depicting the table and the background, while the figures of the three angels are rendered exactly. It is interesting, however, that the central angel bears a cross nimbus with the inscribed words "He who is."[8]

The Trinity Church of the Makhrishchski Monastery, to which Sergii for a time withdrew after a disagreement between him and his brother Stefan, before he built a new monastery in the wilderness on the river Kershchach, possessed a detailed, nearly full-size (114 x 111.5 cm) copy of Rublev's *Trinity* (plate 21).[9] Here, too, the three angels especially are copied faithfully, while the table and the background are depicted more freely. So far as one can tell, the central angel has no cross nimbus.

6 Cited by Müller, op. cit., pp. 45f.

7 Ibid., p. 46.

8 Thus, a reversion back to the type of Trinity icon in which the central figure is identified by the divine name, and therefore identified with Christ—Trans.

9 This icon is differently dated: Lebedewa, *Andrej Rubljow* (p. 124), to the thirties or forties of the fifteenth century (so older than Paissii's copy), Kyslassowa, *Russische Ikonen* (plate 45) to the first half or middle of the sixteenth century.

71

PLATE 20

Icon from the Cathedral of the Dormition in the Monastery of St Joseph of Volokalamsk;
Monk Paissii; 1484/5; Museum Andrei Rublev, Moscow.

PLATE 21

Icon from the Church of the Trinity of the Makhrishchskii Monastery; Historical Museum, Moscow; first half of sixteenth century.

Given the way Rublev's *Trinity* has been greatly treasured since the fifteenth century, it makes one wonder that the oldest sources have nothing to say about its development and, indeed, scarcely mention it at all as an individual work. As far as records are concerned, the icon is first mentioned at the Stoglav Council of 1551, which singles out Andrei Rublev, along with the ancient Greek masters, as a canonical model for the depiction of the Holy Trinity. This reference has, in the meantime, been so relativized that it is may be possible that what was referred to is not the icon so well known today, but other depictions of this theme from the hand of Rublev. Yet, it is clear that no other *Trinity* was ever ascribed to Rublev and that the copies, from the fifteenth century onwards, all go back to the Rublev's famous icon at the Trinity-Sergii Monastery.

A further witness to the ever-growing fame of Rublev's *Trinity* is provided by the "Account of the Holy Icon-Painters," compiled about 1700. It contains no independent ancient traditions, but draws together (with varying degrees of success) facts from well-known written sources. This goes for the frequently over-valued notice that Rublev had, on Nikon's orders, painted an icon of the Holy Trinity "In honour of his [that is, Nikon's] holy father, the wonderworker Sergii." The notice is excerpted from Pachomii's *Life of Nikon,* in which, however, the reference is not to the Trinity icon, but to a second church of the Trinity, built in stone, which Nikon had erected over the grave of Sergii.[10]

❧

The circumstances of the development of Rublev's *Trinity* are only indirectly revealed in the oldest sources. On Nikon's orders, Andrei Rublev, a monk of the Andronikov Monastery in Moscow, had together with his old friend Daniil magnificently painted the stone Church of the Trinity in the St Sergii Monastery between the years 1422 and 1427. Because this was the last work of the two painter-monks, and likewise their spiritual and artistic testament, as the *Life of Nikon* asserts, and since Rublev had never before worked in the St Sergii Monastery, the icon of the Trinity must have been painted at that time, together with the still-extant iconostasis.

One can further conclude that it was meant to be where a faithful copy stands today—to the right of the royal doors of the icon screen[11]—and not, as has sometimes been concluded from the notice of the "Account of the Holy Icon-Painters" as an epitaph at the grave of the saint, which is found today in the Church of the Trinity on the right-hand wall close to the icon screen.

Despite its secondary character, Pachomii the Serb doubtless hits upon a truth when he recorded that Rublev painted his *Trinity* "in honour of the holy father Sergii." For if he, as the spokesman for Sergii's community of monks, wrote that Nikon had caused his Church of the Trinity to be built over the grave of the saint—for whatever other reasons—"in praise and remembrance of his father," then this would apply to its whole decoration. And, which icon with greater right served not only the glorification of the Holy Trinity but also the "praise and remembrance" of Sergii of Radonezh than the icon, dedicated to the mystery that wonderfully surrounded the whole life of this "chosen vessel," this "dwelling-place of the Holy Trinity"?

10 Cf. Müller, *Dreifaltigkeitsikone,* p. 46f.

11 I.e., in place of the icon of Jesus Christ, which usually occupies this position—Trans.

74

CHAPTER SIX

The Spirit of Truth

The Trinitarian mysticism of St Sergii of Radonezh and his school, in which we have recognized the theological and spiritual background of St Andrei Rublev's *Trinity*, is embedded in the spirit and tradition of the Orthodox Church. It is not accidental that in the fourteenth century this tradition had experienced a powerful revival of the mystical movement that became known in history as "hesychasm." Since lively relations existed between Russia and the Mother Church of Byzantium—Sergii had, for example, introduced the coenobitic rule into his monastery on the express decree and wish of the Œcumenical Patriarch—the saint might well have heard of the discussion that this movement had unleashed.[1]

Sergii was no learned theologian in the modern sense of the word, and he is not likely to have had much grasp of the difficult, technical aspects of the dogmatic issues of his time. At the time, a great stir had been created by the teaching of St Gregory of Palamas (1296–1349) on the real distinction in God between his uncreated, unknowable essence (*ousia*) and the uncreated, but knowable energies (*energeiai*) in which participation is possible. The hesychast controversy renewed and concentrated attention on the question always of the deepest concern for every believing Christian and, especially, for every monk: How can a creature partake in the "general grace of the Holy Trinity"?[2] How can humankind find access to the Father, who "dwells in unapproachable light, that no one has seen or can see" (1 Tim 6.16)?

The answer of Scripture and tradition is unambiguous: "No one knows the Son, save the Father, and no one knows the Father, save the Son and the one to whom the Son wills to reveal him" (Matt 11.27). Therefore, "no one comes to the Father, save through" the Son (Jn 14.6), and "no one can come to" the Son, "except the Father draws him" (Jn 6.44), and "gives" him this coming (Jn 6.65). But the one through whom the Father reveals the Son and through whom he draws human kind to the Son is the same: the Holy Spirit, "who proceeds from the Father" (Jn 15.26), but comes to us through the Son (Jn 14.26). It is he, and he alone, who makes possible the confession of the Son as Lord (1 Cor 12.3), for he "takes" from the Son and "glorifies" him (Jn 16.14); he "bears witness" of him (Jn 15.26) and causes the disciples to "remember all that he has said to them" (Jn 14.26). For this is the task of the "abiding Paraclete," whom the Son has sent from the Father in his stead: as the "Spirit of sonship" (Rom 8.15), "to abide" with the disciples "for ever" (Jn 14.16), and to unite them with the Son, who alone ensures their access to the Father. Only the one who has received the grace of the Holy Spirit will become a living "dwelling place of the Father and the Son" (Jn 14.23). We have received this

1 See Vasiliev, "Andrei Rublev and Gregory Palamas," and Bushkovitch, "Limits of Hesychasm."

2 Florensky, *The Trinity–St Sergius Lavra and Russia*, p. 17.

"Spirit from God" in holy baptism, which, from being sons of the old Adam, makes us "sons of God" in Christ thanks to the grace of "adoption as sons," indeed makes us "partakers of the divine nature" (2 Pet 1.4).

❧

In this context, St Gregory Palamas, too, taught that the divine essence is inaccessible to the creature. Only the three consubstantial persons partake in the All-holy Trinity; yet "the divine and uncreated grace and energy of God is indivisibly divided, like the sun's rays that warm, illumine, quicken and bring increase," and gives a share in the same divine essence.[3] For "the divine and deifying illumination and grace is not the essence but the energy of God,"[4] which is not to be separated from the essence. "Thus it is impossible to participate in God's essence, even for those who are deified by divine grace. It is, however, possible to participate in the divine energy."[5]

Grace is nothing else than the activity of the consubstantial, holy and sanctifying, divine and deifying Holy Spirit. For "the grace of the Spirit, though differing from the divine nature, is not separated from it; rather, it draws those privileged to receive it towards union with the Holy Spirit."[6]

❧

This Spirit, which the believer receives with the anointing of chrism at holy baptism, sets his seal on the whole existence of the believer, the goal of which is, according to the word of Seraphim of Sarov (1759–1833), the conscious "acquisition of the Holy Spirit." What we are accustomed to call "Trinitarian mysticism" is nothing else than the precious fruit of this acquisition of the Holy Spirit.

> As he promised, when the Holy Spirit came upon the apostles, O Christ,
> in his own power, he united the divided tongues of the varied nations in
> the single harmony of faith in the uncreated Trinity. Come and dwell in
> us, too, good lover of human kind, we beseech you.[7]

The Divine Liturgy is the place where this continual coming and activity of the Holy Spirit is manifested in a pre-eminent way. For it is the Spirit, who not only makes the gifts of bread and wine into "the precious body and the precious blood of our Lord Jesus Christ" (Liturgy of St John Chrysostom) but ensures also that the faithful will through these gifts continually have a share anew in the Holy Spirit, and through him in the Son, who is present in the gifts that have been changed, have communion with the Father. Solemnly, the priest thus prays in the Byzantine Liturgy after the "anamnesis" and Christ's words of institution:

> Also we offer you this spiritual worship without shedding of blood, and
> we ask, pray and implore you: send down your Holy Spirit upon us and
> upon these gifts here set forth, and make this bread the precious body of
> your Christ, and what is in this cup the precious blood of your Christ,
> changing them by your Holy Spirit, so that those who partake of them
> may obtain vigilance of soul, forgiveness of sins, communion of your

3 Gregory Palamas, *Capita CL* 68 (*The Philokalia: the Complete Text*, translated by G.E.H. Palmer, Philip Sherrard, and Kallistos Ware, vol. IV, London: Faber & Faber, 1995, p. 377).

4 Ibid., 69 (p. 378).

5 Ibid., 111 (p. 397).

6 Ibid., 108 (p. 395).

7 *Pentekostarion*, Wednesday after Pentecost, Orthros, kathisma 1.

Holy Spirit, fulness of the Kingdom of Heaven, freedom to speak in your presence, not judgment or condemnation.

After the receiving of the Holy Mysteries, the choir sings once again:

We have seen the true light, we have received the heavenly Spirit, we have found the true faith [in the Father], as we worship the undivided Trinity; for the Trinity has saved us.

It is significant that this text is taken from the service for Pentecost, for we owe all this to the self-revelation and self-communication of the triune God, which finds its fulfilment in the descent of the Holy Spirit. What first happened at Pentecost, happens therefore anew in each Divine Liturgy, so that the same fulness of grace is granted to the "last," as to the "first."

❧

Against this background, the whole life of St Sergii of Radonezh appears as a perfect mirror of what it really means to be a Christian. At the baptism of the little Varfolomei, whom the Holy Spirit had already called in his mother's womb, the priest, illumined by the grace of the Holy Spirit, recognized that this child would one day become a chosen vessel of God, a dwelling place and servant of the Holy Trinity.

Gradually, adapting itself to the bodily and spiritual growth of the child, the grace of the Holy Spirit took possession of him. When this future preacher of the Holy Trinity received the holy gifts at his monastic consecration, he was renewed, and in a way perceptible to those who stood around, he was filled with the grace of the Holy Spirit—that same grace also designated as the grace of the Holy Trinity and the activity of the indivisible unity among three divine persons.

In the power of the wonder-working grace of the Holy Spirit, Sergii makes his monastery a dwelling place of the Holy Trinity; a place where he serves the life-giving Trinity and where a great and constantly growing number of monks is clothed by him in the name of the Holy Trinity. Confidently, the biographer of this man graced from his mother's womb—who in a long life, unfolding the grace of holy baptism, had "put off the old man and put on the new human form"— closes his work with these words: "And what he always wished to see he saw: he received from the illumination of the Most Holy Trinity (as it befits one who fasts), the adoration of monks."

❧

A life in communion with the All-holy Trinity in and through the Holy Spirit is the meaning and end of the Christian life: this is, as will become clear to us, the spiritual legacy that St Sergii of Radonezh left to his sons as a living example. As we saw, his first biographer, Epifanii the Wise, had already grasped this, and Pachomii the Serb consistently made this idea the *leitmotiv* of his expanded *Life of St Sergii*. He surely did this not, as we have already emphasized, on his own accord, but simply as a faithful interpreter of the image of the saint that Sergii's disciples had handed down a generation after his death.

This spiritual legacy is not in any way original in the sense of a new personal creation of the saint. Anything like that would have completely distanced him from St Gregory Palamas, the great theologian of the grace of the Holy Spirit. It is, rather, in the best sense of the word, "traditional," as the quintessence of the theological, liturgical, and mystical tradition of the ancient Church, that is, of the Eastern Orthodox Church. One would certainly not go wrong if one thought of the whole of St Sergii's life as the fulfillment of the prayer from the services for Pentecost, which runs like a scarlet thread through all the offices of the Eastern Church:

> O Heavenly King, Comforter, Spirit of Truth, everywhere present, filling all things, Treasury of blessings and Giver of life, Come and abide in us, cleanse us from every stain, and, O Good One, save our souls.

The spirituality of St Sergii of Radonezh was, therefore, so traditional in itself, that the saint appears to be the first—or one of the first—on Russian soil to plant this spirit-filled Trinitarian mysticism, like a precious cutting, in the soil of Slav Christendom, which was to bear rich fruit for centuries.[8] In witness to this are not only the numerous churches dedicated to the Trinity, but also many objects of applied art, including the countless depictions of the hospitality of Abraham, which became one of the most beloved subjects of Russian icon-painting. The Godhead cannot allow itself to be depicted as an image, yet wherever the artist wants to suggest its saving presence, the three guests of Abraham appear—as on the Byzantine miniature of the fourteenth century, in the upper register of the depiction (plate 19). The image of the life-giving Trinity graces countless iconostases, other icons of all kinds, liturgical embroidery, crosses, liturgical vessels, and seven-branched candlesticks, bearing witness in Russia to the glorification of the *mysterium Trinitatis*, which is full of vitality right up to the present.[9]

8 Cf. Florensky, *The Trinity–St Sergius Lavra and Russia*.

9 Cf. the great Jubilee volume, *Troitsa-Sergeieva-Lavra*.

CHAPTER SEVEN

The Heavenly Liturgy

For centuries, Andrei Rublev's icon of the Holy Trinity has had its established place to the right of the royal doors of the iconostasis in Nikon's church, where normally one finds the icon of Christ. Yet, it is also a festal icon: the icon for the feast of Pentecost. But none of this—neither its association with Pentecost, nor its position on the iconostasis—is obvious.

Hitherto, it had been assumed that Rublev's *Troitsa* was originally set up as an epitaph at the grave of St Sergii, yet we can determine no sound reason for this. Most probably, from the beginning the icon was intended for the iconostasis in its present position, where it assumes the place normally occupied by the icon of Christ.[1] The more customary icon of Christ the Pantocrator is to be found to its right. Interesting to note in the same iconostasis is an early copy of Rublev's *Troitsa*, located to the left of the icon of the Mother of God, which occupies its traditional place to the left of the royal doors (cf. plate 22).

Because the ancient feasts of the Church were all memorials of particular events in the history of salvation, for centuries neither West nor East had a proper feast of the Holy Trinity. In Rome, it was first introduced, against fierce opposition, as a universal feast by Pope John XXII in 1334; even today, though, the East knows no such feast expressly dedicated to this, the deepest of all the mysteries of the faith. In Russia, however, Pentecost acquired with time the character of a feast of the Holy Trinity. It has often been assumed, probably with good reason, that this happened under the influence of the Trinitarian mysticism of St Sergii of Radonezh,[2] the fullest pictorial expression of which is found in Rublev's *Troitsa*.

Through this link between Pentecost and the *mysterium Trinitatis*, whereby Pentecost became the Feast of the Holy Trinity, Rublev's Trinity icon and other similar icons equally attain the rank of a festal icon. The descent of the Holy Spirit is celebrated by the Orthodox Church on the following day, with its own icon and, above all, in the texts that occur throughout the services for Pentecost.

A careful reading of the liturgical texts makes clear that the emergence of this feast of the Holy Trinity was not at all a new phenomenon, but rather a deepening of the festal mystery of Pentecost. One might see this as a shifting of emphasis from the history of salvation to theology. As Pentecost commemorates first of all the saving event of the outpouring of the Holy Spirit, promised by Christ, so the liturgical texts teach precisely that this fulness and fulfilment of the Paschal mystery also designates equally the fulness of God's self-revelation.

> We celebrate Pentecost, and the advent of the Spirit, and the appointed time of the promise, and the fulfilment of hope. What a mystery! How great and how august! Therefore we cry to you: Creator of all, Lord, glory to you![3]

1 This place is taken by icons of the Trinity in many other churches, many of which are not dedicated to the Holy Trinity.

2 Florensky, *The Trinity–St Sergius Lavra and Russia*, p. 25. For more detail, see p. 67.

3 *Pentekostarion*, Pentecost, Great Vespers, sticheron 1.

In the Prophets you proclaimed to us the way of salvation, and in the Apostles, O our Saviour, the grace of your Spirit shone forth; you, O God, are the first, and you are after all these things, too, and you are our God to the ages.[4]

Come, O people, let us worship the three-personed God, the Son in the Father with the Holy Spirit; for the Father begat timelessly the coeternal Son who reigns with him, and the Holy Spirit was in the Father, glorified with the Son, one power, one being, one Godhead, worshipping whom we all say: Holy God, who created all things through your Son, with the cooperation of the Holy Spirit. Holy Strong, through whom we know the Father and through whom the Holy Spirit is present in the cosmos. Holy Immortal, the Comforter Spirit, who proceeds from the Father and rests in the Son. Holy Trinity, glory to you.[5]

As once the zealous one, breathing fire, rejoiced to ride the burning chariot of fire, so now he manifests his radiant inspiration from on high upon the Apostles, illumined by which they made known to all the Trinity.[6]

Light is the Father, light the Son, light the Holy Spirit, which was sent in tongues of flame upon the Apostles, and through whom the whole world is initiated in the light, to reverence the Holy Trinity.[7]

❧

Therefore, Pentecost is naturally the feast of the fulness of God's gift of grace, which the Holy Spirit, "God and deifying," brings about in the faithful.

The Holy Spirit provides everything; he makes prophecy abound, he perfects priests, he taught wisdom to the unlearned, and showed fishermen to be theologians, he fashions the whole ordinance of the Church. Consubstantial, and sharing sovereignty, with the Father and the Son, Comforter, glory to you.[8]

In your courts, O Lord, we the faithful bow the knee of our soul and body, we raise hymns to you, the Father without beginning, and the Son equally without beginning, and the coeternal and all-holy Spirit, who gives light and holiness to our souls.[9]

Thus spake the reverend and august mouth: you will not experience absence, friends. For when I have ascended to the most high, paternal throne, I shall pour out the abundant grace of the Spirit to enlighten those who long for him.[10]

Renew the longed-for and righteous Spirit in us, that we may possess him eternally in our inmost parts, the One who, proceeding from the Father, is always united with him, who burns up the pollution of hateful matter and, O Almighty, purges the stains from our mind.[11]

4 Ibid., sticheron 5.

5 Ibid., dogmatikon.

6 Ibid., Orthros, first canon, ode 9, troparion 1.

7 Ibid., exapostilarion 2.

8 Ibid., Great Vespers, sticheron 3.

9 Ibid., sticheron 7.

10 Ibid., Orthros, iambic canon, ode 1, troparion 1.

11 Ibid., ode 6, troparion 1.

As many as breathe the grace that flows from God are enlightened, become radiant, and are changed into a strange, most majestic form. Knowing the undivided equal Wisdom, we glorify the threefold essence.[12]

❧

Old humanity was afflicted by fragmentation, a consequence of that "confusion of tongues" that God had decreed as punishment for pride in the building of the Tower of Babel. The new humanity offers praise in the multitude of languages thanks to the one Spirit of God, renewed out of a single mouth. Similarly with the knowledge of the mystery of the triune God, the Holy Spirit brings about a new graced unity among the faithful, and of the faithful with God, the model of which is the Unity in Three Persons of God himself (as Evagrios Pontikos put it in his *Letter on Faith*).

> Once tongues were confused because of the effrontery of the making of the tower; now tongues are made wise through the glory of the knowledge of God. There God condemned the ungodly for their fault; here Christ enlightens the fishermen with the Spirit. Then dissonance came about as a punishment; now harmony is renewed for the salvation of our souls.[13]

> The presence of the power of the Holy Spirit divinely unites into one divine harmony the voice shattered of old because of an evil consonance, bringing the faithful to understand and know the Trinity, in which we are established.[14]

> When the Most High came down and confused the tongues, he parted the nations. When he divided out the tongues of fire, he called all to unity; and with one voice we glorify the All-holy Spirit.[15]

> Apart from the laws of nature, a strange thing has been heard, for the one voice of the disciples resounds with the grace of the Spirit, and peoples, tribes and tongues learn by hearing about the mighty acts of God, initiated in the knowledge of the Trinity.[16]

❧

The great themes of the Feast of Pentecost—knowledge of the triune being of God, sanctification and deification, reunion of once fragmented humanity through the fulness of the Spirit poured out on the Apostles—radiate from the liturgical texts. They are the same great theological themes that imprinted themselves on Sergii of Radonezh and his disciples in their Trinitarian mysticism, indeed on all those inspired by the spirit of the liturgy. Here, it is sufficient for us to maintain that Rublev's icon of the Holy Trinity—precisely where it originally stood—from the very beginning had its theological meaning in the mystery of Pentecost.

❧

12 Ibid., ode 9, troparion 2.

13 Ibid., of Great Vespers, doxastikon of the aposticha.

14 Ibid., Orthros, first canon, ode 3, troparion.

15 Pentecost kontakion (translation from *The Divine Liturgy of Our Father among the Saints John Chrysostom*, Oxford University Press, 1995, p. 78).

16 *Pentekostarion*, Pentecost, first canon, ode 9, troparion 2.

The theological place of the icon is not, first of all, private devotion, but the celebration of the Divine Liturgy. Like the icon, the liturgy is, in its essence, a recollection making present what God has done for his people. It is, therefore, not so much a human celebration as it is an earthly copy and reflection of the heavenly liturgy—a human concelebration with the heavenly powers. From the earliest times, accounts of angels celebrating the liturgy together with the saints are, therefore, not at all rare. Of Sergii, too, it is said:

> Some time when Feodor was already consecrated in the abode of the Venerable Sergii, Saint Sergii celebrated the Divine Liturgy with the afore-mentioned Stefan, his brother according to the flesh, and this Feodor his relative was with him, and the afore-mentioned Isakii the Silent was standing in the church. He was, as I mentioned before, a very virtuous man and because of this he saw a revelation. He saw at the altar a fourth man concelebrating with them: a very wonderful man whose sight was strange and indescribable, shining with great brightness in the face and with radiating vestments. And during the little entrance that angelic-like and wonderful man came out after the saint and his face was shining like the sun so that it was impossible to look at him. His vestments were unusual, wonderful, shiny, so that they looked like they were of golden designs.[17]

Not without hesitation, after the liturgy Sergii replied to his disciples' question as to who this wonderful celebrant was:

> Oh, my beloved children! If the Lord God revealed it to you, can I conceal it? What you saw was an Angel of the Lord and not only on this day, but always, through God's visitation, I, unworthy one, celebrate the liturgy with him. But tell no one what you have seen as long as I live.[18]

This thought of the heavenly-earthly concelebration, which determines the whole Orthodox church building and its iconographic decoration, finds beautiful expression in the Cherubic Hymn, which the choir sings at the Great Entrance, the festal procession of the Holy Gifts from the table of preparation to the altar:

> We, who in a mystery represent the Cherubim and sing the thrice-holy hymn to the life-giving Trinity, let us now lay aside every care of this life. For we are about to receive the King of all, invisibly escorted by the angelic hosts. Alleluia, alleluia, alleluia.

It is not to be forgotten that Sergii, while still in his mother's womb, had at this song cried out as a prophetic witness to the fact that he himself would one day become a "servant and a dwelling-place of the Holy Trinity."

17 Klimenko, The "Vita," p. 166 (Hackel, Sergij von Radonesh, p. 131).

18 Fedotov, Treasury of Russian Spirituality, p. 77 (with slight modification; Hackel, Sergij von Radonesh, p. 132; cf. Klimenko, The "Vita," p. 167, where there seems to be a lacuna).

❧

The deep-rooted knowledge that the earthly liturgy reflects the heavenly, and the overwhelming consciousness of the living presence of the threefold God, determines not only the liturgical texts but also the whole structure of the church building and the performance of the sacred actions of the Orthodox Church.

The church building is always "orientated," that is, its apse faces east, and the altar, or sanctuary, is found in the eastern part of the church. This has a deep biblical and symbolic sense. According to the teaching of the Bible (Gen 2.8), the Garden of Eden, Paradise, and therefore the place prepared by God for the first human beings, lay to the East, towards the rising of the sun. The fallen human beings were punished by being driven from this Paradise, and a cherub with a flaming sword kept watch "at the east of the garden of Eden . . . to guard the way to the tree of life" (Gen 3.24). Only through the Cross and Resurrection of Christ has Paradise become open again to humankind.

> Unbroken you preserved the seals, O Christ, in your rising from the tomb, nor did you injure the locks of the virgin womb in your birth, and you have opened to us the portals of Paradise.[19]

> A sacred Pascha has been revealed to us today, a new and holy Pascha, a mystic Pascha, an all-venerable Pascha, a Pascha that is Christ the Redeemer, an unblemished Pascha, a great Pascha, a Pascha of the faithful, a Pascha that has opened for us the gates of Paradise, a Pascha that makes all the faithful holy.[20]

> Through your resurrection, O Lord, the universe has been enlightened, and Paradise is again opened. The whole creation sings your praises and each day offers you a hymn.[21]

The believer in Christ only finally enters this Paradise, his original homeland, at the moment of death (Lk 23.43); before that time, he lives through faith in his Redeemer and in the hope of the salvation that has already been secured for him. Thus, the liturgy and the space in which it is celebrated have the task of making sacramentally present this living tension between promise and fulfilment.

So the sanctuary in the apse of the church symbolizes the "Holy Place," the place where Christ's sacrifice on the Cross is made present, the "Paradise in the East"; the place of longing for each of the faithful, to which they always turn to offer their prayers. Now, this space is not yet immediately accessible to the Christian. The icon screen, into which the ancient altar screen has grown in the East, cuts off even his gaze. It is the icons on the screen that now bring God's great acts of salvation to the understanding of the faithful and communicate them to their "memory." This applies to the whole church year, which symbolizes our existence *in via*. At Pascha (Easter), however, all the doors of the sanctuary are opened wide as a sign that through Christ's resurrection the entrance to Paradise has been opened.

Therefore, it is deeply significant that the Christian always prays facing east. As a believer, he stands in the Spirit before the door—in principle the open door—of Paradise and its Tree of Life in the expectation that the Lord will open to him for ever the door to the "house of the Father." For it is *from the* East that he looks for the coming of his Lord at the second, glorious *Parousia*; it is *in the East* that the "sun of righteousness" (Mal 4.2) will arise, whose first "rising" (Lk 1.78) is the cause of his salvation.

For the common prayer of clergy and faithful in the Divine Liturgy the priest

19 Paschal Canon, ode 6, troparion 1 (translated by Archimandrite Ephrem [Lash], *The Services of the Holy and Great Sunday of Pascha*, St Andrew's Monastery, Manchester 2000, pp. 8f.).

20 Easter, Lauds, stichera 1 (op. cit., p. 18).

21 Monday of Renewal [Easter Monday], Vespers, sticheron 2.

also, as in former days in the Western Church, stands facing east, for "prayer," according to the definition of Clement of Alexandria and other Fathers, is a "conversation of the spirit with God." So, through this common "standing before the Lord" the impression will be avoided that in the liturgy—apart from isolated appeals and greetings—it is rather a matter of a dialogue between clergy and people. For prayer is not a dialogue between human beings, but a dialogue between the people of God, gathered together, and their Lord.

As was once also in the Western Church, not only the faithful but also the celebrating priest stand at the offering of the unbloody sacrifice before the altar, facing east, an analogy with the heavenly high priest, Christ, who for us constantly enters into the heavenly sanctuary with the Father through his own blood (Hebrews). All this is to be heeded in the interpretation of Rublev's *Troitsa*, which clearly presupposes a liturgical scenario.

CHAPTER EIGHT

Tradition and the New Creation

When in the first half of the fifteenth century Andrei Rublev received from Nikon the commission to paint an icon of the Holy Trinity, he was not venturing on to new territory. Throughout the realm of Byzantine culture, there had been such icons for centuries, even in Russia, and they were well known to Rublev. Yet the iconographic tradition was, as we have seen, not unambiguous, a state of affairs that did not satisfy everyone. A question to this effect, posed at the so-called Stoglav Synod (1551), applied equally to the time of Rublev.

> On icons of the Holy Trinity, some represent a cross in the nimbus of only the middle figure, others on all three. On ancient and on Greek icons, the words "Holy Trinity" are written at the top, but there is a cross in the nimbus of any of the three. At present, "IC XC" and "the Holy Trinity" are written next to the central figure. Consult the sacred canons and tell us which practice one should follow. The Reply: painters must paint icons according to the ancient models, as the Greeks painted them, as Andrei Rublev and other renowned painters made them. The inscription should be: "the Holy Trinity." Painters are in no way to use their imaginations.[1]

Because the Greek masters had developed different types of the icon, the iconography of the *Troitsa* continued to be ambiguous. The fact that there was no model established in all the details allowed the painters considerable freedom in painting the icon this way or that, as they pleased. One could say, not to put too fine a point on it, that no icon could be called *the* icon of the Trinity. To a certain degree, each icon painter could, in complete faithfulness to the tradition, exercise some creativity.

It would be fascinating to place a large number of icons of the Trinity side by side and observe which aspects of the theme each painter had wanted to bring out. It would then become apparent how one of them had the promise of the birth of Isaac in mind, another the sacrifice of Isaac, yet another the consubstantiality of the three divine persons, an aspect that, again, could be brought out in various different ways. Our question is, then, how Rublev availed himself of this existing freedom without in the least breaching the limits of the tradition.

The iconographic tradition, so far as it comes under our consideration, had evolved, in the Byzantine and late-Byzantine periods, essentially two types, both

1 Stoglav Synod, canon 41.1 (cited from L. Ouspensky, *Theology of the Icon*, trans. A. Gythiel, vol. 2, Crestwood, NY: St Vladimir's Seminary Press, 1992, p. 291).

of which Rublev was most likely aware. The distinction between them was primarily formal but was also a matter of content, as the title of the icons makes clear.

Through his master, Feofan Grek, Rublev had been entrusted with the older
christological type. The main characteristic of this type is that the central angel,
identified by a variety of attributes as Christ, the Son, always completely dominates the picture. He faces the beholder, who looks directly towards him, the other
angels being simply accompanying figures, who are often depicted as smaller.
Regardless of the title of the icon, we are formally dealing with an icon of Christ,
a distant echo of the early Christian, christological interpretation of Gen 18.

In the case of the Greek icons, several of which existed in Russia at all periods, Rublev was, moreover, aware of a more recent, more formally Trinitarian
type. Here, the three angels are as similar one to another as possible. Attitude,
gesture, and posture of the angels are now very marked and allow one to recognize relationships of interaction. This is achieved mainly through the abandon-
ment of the frontal view, even though the central angel still looks directly at the
beholder. While the christological type retains the biblical background (house,
tree, and so on), the Trinitarian type often replaces this with a richly developed
architectural setting.

If one compares Rublev's *Troitsa* with its predecessors, then it becomes
immediately apparent that it reproduces simply neither the one nor the other
type. The form of composition is essentially that of the Trinitarian type, with
these striking modifications:

• The central angel no longer looks at the beholder but at the angel on the
left. Because the gaze of the angel on the left and that of the angel on the right
cross one another, the centre of gravity moves from the central angel to the one
on the left.

• This impression is strengthened because the angels at each side are of the
same size as the one in the middle. This distinguishes Rublev's *Troitsa*, too, from
the icons that immediately preceded it in the Trinity Monastery.

• From the christological type, Rublev gives the angel in the middle the clothing characteristic of Christ and adds an unusual feature: the golden *clavus* (sewn
on stripe). Moreover, he makes the clothing of the other two angels unique and
not interchangeable.

• The gestures of the three angels are essentially those of the Trinitarian type,
yet with striking modifications. Originally, the play of the hands was motivated
by the objects on the table. The central angel pointed to the great chalice in the
middle of the table; the angel on the left blessed the chalice-bowl standing before
him; and the angel on the right stretched out hands towards what was in the bowl
standing before him or towards a piece of bread on the table. These gestures
appear in the icons that immediately precede Rublev's *Troitsa*. However, in
Rublev's icon the table is so small and the figures are so close together that there
is no room for any other vessels except for the great chalice in the middle of
the table. The table is bare apart from this bowl. Over this bowl (see frontispiece),
the right hand of the central angel points. The angel on the left raises his right
hand both pointing and blessing in the direction of the angel on the right, who
for his part drops his hand to the table, a movement that reflects the inclination
of his head.

Although still in keeping with traditional elements, these gestures clearly express another meaning. They now no longer relate to the food but, in an individual way, to the persons. In short, Rublev has not simply re-created another icon with christological interpretation: one individual form with two companions; neither has he created what could be considered a standard Trinitarian icon, that is, three equal, interchangeable forms. Rather, he has shown three non-interchangeable persons.

• The table has lost its character as a dining table, still retained in the preceding icons (note the tablecloth), and has become a white cube on which is found nothing save a great chalice-bowl with the head of a calf. The way the side of the cube that faces the beholder has developed from the table as constructed in previous icons into a right-angled opening renders this table recognizable as an altar. From ancient times, an opening on the east side of the altar for the keeping of relics and for the reserving of the Eucharist has been the norm (as it once was in the West).[2]

• The hosts, Abraham and Sarah, who already in the Trinitarian type of icon have been retained as barely more than accompanying figures, have disappeared. As with the servant and the calf, there is no longer room for them.

• Instead of the architectural background characteristic of the Trinitarian type, Rublev has, like his immediate predecessors, gone back to the biblical background, although reducing its size considerably. The angel on the left is co-ordinated with a house, the one in the middle with a tree, and the one on the right with a rock; in the preceding icons, the house and the rock had been interchanged. The reduction of these elements and their relationship to each of the three figures lifts them from the context of narrative into that of symbol.

❧

In comparison with the older models available to him, Rublev seems to have radically simplified the subject by consciously reducing everything to essentials. Such a concentration on essentials was hitherto found only in miniatures, where everything is conditioned by the form (often a round disc) and its limited size.[3] By means of its size, Rublev's icon raises the essential to the monumental. Yet, there is nothing coarse about his rendering of the subject: rather, the little that he has depicted is painted with the greatest care and with almost courtly elegance.

If one gives wing for a moment to a fantasy, inspired by St Iosif of Volokalamsk's account of Rublev and his friend Daniil, then it is not difficult to imagine how the humble monk Andrei sat on a chair for hours in contemplation of an icon of the Holy Trinity, perhaps the very icon his was to replace; how he took pains, lifting his eyes to the material colours of the icon, to raise his spiritual eyes to the immaterial and divine light of which the icon is an earthly reflection. As he wrestled to grasp the truth that was proclaimed in the Old Testament model, we can see his countenance change as the immaterial and divine light broke into his soul and filled him with an unspeakable divine joy because he had now beheld what he had to paint.

❧

2 J. Braun, *Die christliche Altar*, Munich 1924, vol. 1, pp. 237ff.

3 See the many *panagia* depicted in Vzdornov, *Dreifaltigkeit Andrej Rubljovs*.

As we have seen, Rublev proceeded in his work very traditionally and was content to make small, often overlooked modifications to his models. Even in this he demonstrates not only his artistic mastery, but also his true genius as a painter of icons. The principal task of the icon painter is not to make something new that dumbfounds the beholder and leaves him often perplexed. New iconographic types—icons manifest for the first time—are rare, comparatively speaking. With church proclamation in general, which the icon painter serves in his own way, the icon painter takes part in the task of "keeping the good thing committed [to us]" (2 Tim 1.14). The more faithfully he does this in his time and with the resources of his time, the more selflessly he "holds fast to the traditions" received (1 Cor 11.2). The more purely he adheres to church tradition and proclamation, so much the more will he, after the example of the great teachers of the Church, paradoxically become genuinely creative. The iconographer does not change the language, which would make him altogether incomprehensible in his own time and for posterity, but he releases unsuspected depths and gives them expression so as to make them accessible to others.

Rublev's *Troitsa* lends itself to being understood in exemplary fashion, for, in contrast to so much religious art, even of the first rank, it has lost nothing of its power of religious expression. On the contrary, one has the impression that over the course of the centuries it has even more to say.

Despite his modifications, Rublev was not at all original. Rather, his genius consisted in advancing the ancient iconographic tradition of his Church to a depth and transparent clarity that had never been attained before or even later, even in the most exact copies. This is the place where the personality of the painter enters permanently into his work. The ancient sources about the monk Andrei draw attention to his great humility, which more than his artistic genius led not only to the canonization of his *Troitsa* at the synod of 1551, but also to his official glorification as a saint in 1988 as part of the celebrations of the millennium of Russian Christianity.

For without a deeply rooted humility, a complete renunciation of all worldly ambition before the sublimity of the mystery that he served as a painter, Rublev would never have been able to paint his *Trinity*. Not once did he set his name as icon painter to his work.

CHAPTER NINE

Essence and Person

The question about the relationship between the three angels and the three persons of the Trinity, whom they symbolize, is a modern one and has been the subject of much discussion.[1] In this discussion, the angels have been identified with each of the three divine persons, presupposing that such an identification of the three angels is possible. However, in doing so, it has been overlooked that in the whole iconographic tradition, including that immediately accessible to Rublev, only one angel has been placed in relation to one of the persons of the Trinity, if at all; namely—and without exception—the central angel as Christ.

Therefore, if one assumes, as we have done, that Rublev consciously departed from the iconographic tradition in that he relates each of the three divine persons to a particular angel, then one must point to some clues in the representation itself. The first of such evidence has been detailed in the preceding chapter. The elements that Rublev chose from the older tradition and the way and manner in which he modified them and gave them significance create the impression that he deliberately wanted to give each particular figure an unmistakeable countenance. In this chapter, we will delineate more such clues.

This question as to the identity of the three angelic forms—however fruitless it may be in the case of the predecessors of Rublev and also of most of his followers—is, therefore, in his case not only justified, but even unavoidable, if one wants to understand the particular message of his icon. When considering how Rublev meant to have his angels identified, we shall have to set out firmly established evidence, if we are not arbitrarily to introduce into the icon ideas essentially foreign to it.

The real question, of course, is what the icon as a whole expresses. Here, too, opinions vary widely. To some, the icon expresses the timeless mystery of the intra-Trinitarian relationships between the Father, Son, and Spirit, that is, the *theological* Trinity; others see the icon as expressing the eternal decision to send the Son, that is, the *economic* Trinity; still others see in the icon the mystery of the holy Eucharist and the continuing role of the three divine persons in this sacramental making present of the sacrifice of the Son: the *liturgical-eucharistic* Trinity, one could say. The circle of themes extends still further, if one starts from sociological or other premises instead of theological ones. Each premise leads to another identification of the three persons and to another interpretation of the whole picture. We must therefore ask whether there are clues that enable us to decide what Rublev himself wanted to express. This presupposes that we know what he—in response to the essence of the icon—was able to express.

1 Cf. on this in detail Eckhardt ("Dreifaltigkeit-sikone Rublevs"), who is concerned to reduce any attempt at identification *ad absurdum*; Mainka, "Rublevs Dreifaltigkeit-sikone" (1962), as well as Müller, *Dreifaltigkeitsikone*, pp. 60–99, work through all mathematically possible identifications of all the three figures.

❧

Before considering what Rublev was trying to express in the painting of his icon, we need to consider some other circumstances that affect the reading of the icon. If one looks at Rublev's *Troitsa* where it is presented to visitors, in the Tretyakov Gallery in Moscow, one would see a work of art without any authentic context. It is forgotten that the theological place of the icon is the liturgy—in the broadest sense. Normally, each icon of this format not only has its set place within the church building, but also its position in the church year. In the case of the *Troitsa*, its place in the church is to the right of the central doors of the iconostasis, and its place in the church year is the Feast of Pentecost. In particular, its character as a festal icon should not to be overlooked.

Also, we need to remember that the original iconographic representation of the welcoming of Abraham's three guests is as part of the Abraham cycle, which was used as a decorative theme in churches (e.g., S. Maria Maggiore). Examples of this can also be found in the post-iconoclast period (e.g., in Sicily and in S. Marco, Venice). As we have already noted, however, this scene is very early on set free from this context in the history of salvation in order to be placed in a straight-forwardly christological-typological context, together with other Old Testament pictures (e.g., S. Vitale).

From the tenth century onwards, we notice an ever greater autonomy in the depiction of Abraham's three guests, now always appearing as angels. The title, too, is new: "The Holy Trinity." Abraham and Sarah, originally hosts to the main figures of the event, are changed into suppliants of the mystery of the Trinity. The firm context in the history of salvation is no longer set forth. The motif of the hospitality of Abraham now finds a manifold application—apart from examples of art in miniature (seals, manuscripts)—in sanctuary areas (east conches) and monastic refectories (again east conches). The primordial typological (such as in S. Vitale) link to the New Testament mystery of the Divine Liturgy is in both cases clear. From the fourteenth century onwards, Abraham and Sarah may even completely vanish. There remain only the three angels as a pure Old Testament type of the "God of the Christians."

In Russia, alone, a final, highly significant shift of emphasis takes place: the hospitality of Abraham finds itself back once again in a new—but this time New Testament—context in the history of salvation. Pentecost, which already had its own festal theme and festal icon—the descent of the Holy Spirit in the form of tongues of flame on Mary and the twelve Apostles—becomes, in accord with some of the theological texts of the festal office overall, the feast of the fulness of the revelation of the triune God. When and where exactly this shift took place, and what role St Sergii of Radonezh played in it—directly or indirectly—is a question for historians and liturgical scholars to clarify.[2] It is, however, a fact that from this time forward the representation of the Holy Trinity in the form of Abraham's three angelic visitors becomes the festal icon of Pentecost .

❧

2 Hints about this are found in Florensky, *The Trinity–St Sergius Lavra and Russia*, pp. 26f.

A further reason for the contradictory interpretations to which Rublev's *Trinity* has been subjected lies in the fact that the modern beholder proceeds entirely unconsciously from the assumption that his own perspective or point of view is

PLATE 22

Copy of the original Rublev *Trinity*, completed in 1598;
iconostasis of the Church of the Trinity in the Trinity-St Sergii Lavra, Sergiev Posad.

also that of the painter or the icon. This assumption is seemingly required by the geometrical figures—essentially, the circle, the quadrilateral and the triangle—which underlie the structure of the icon.[3] For it seems in contradiction to natural perception to see in the central figure anyone other than the principal person, the Father. Different and contradictory arguments for the identification of the other two angels are often offered.

But what if the seemingly obvious and natural point of view of the beholder is not at all that of the icon? What if, on the contrary, as with ancient depictions of liturgical matters, this scene of a meal is based on inverse perspective, in such a manner that the foreground of the picture in reality lies behind, so that the beholder sees something face-to-face that he can actually only see from behind? What if the icon, therefore, secures for the viewer an insight into the event—and this is indeed its essence—that would otherwise not be accessible to him at all?

A final difficulty is posed, in part, by the poor state of preservation of the icon. Since 1904, the icon has been restored several times and, in part, freed from ancient over-paintings. A copy from the year 1598, which can be found to the left in the same iconostasis at the Trinity Monastery, the painter of which obviously followed the original in all respects, allows us to see what the original composition looked like (plate 22).

A comparison between the original and the copy shows that the background has been essentially preserved. Only the rock behind the angel on the right seems originally to have displayed a crack, which other, older copies even more clearly brought out. It is important, too, that the table is completely clear apart from a single chalice, and not cluttered with any other vessels. Because the gilding of the *nimbi* on the original has not been preserved, it is important to notice that the copy of the central angel has only a simple nimbus, not a cross nimbus, as does the monk Paissii's copy.[4]

Uniquely on the right hand of the central angel the restorers have preserved an ancient modification that appears on all copies, which regrettably has not been corrected: Originally the hand was closed except for the index finger, which pointed to the angel on the right.[5]

In this chapter, we will, first of all, attempt to clarify what Rublev could have depicted and, consequently, what, in all probability, he actually wanted to depict. The painter could not have depicted, if he remained faithful to the essence of the icon, the intra-Trinitarian mystery as such, that is, the so-called theological Trinity. The begetting of the Son from the Father and the procession of the Holy Spirit are ineffable and therefore not capable of depiction, not even in a symbol, for they are completely inexpressible.

Moreover, even if "Christ our God was certainly circumscribable in the flesh, yet his Godhead was withheld from the painter,"[6] how much more so with the unfathomable being of the Holy Trinity! In other words, only that can be depicted which has been manifest to us and has equally, therefore, circumscribed itself.

3 Cf. Mainka, *Rublev's Dreifaltigkeitsikone* (1986), p. 37; Müller, *Dreifaltigkeitsikone*, pp. 54f.

4 Cf. n. 5.

5 This Müller, *Dreifaltigkeitsikone*, p. 67, has thankfully indicated.

6 Stoglav, ch. 43.

Existing uncircumscribed in your divine nature, in the last days you thought fit to become flesh and to be circumscribed, for by the addition of the flesh you assumed all its properties. Therefore by making an imprint of your form, we embrace it relatively, and are lifted up to your love, and from it we draw the grace of healings, following the divine traditions of the Apostles.[7]

Father and Spirit, however, did not become human— the Holy Trinity as such has not been manifest to us. What once appeared before Abraham in human form was only an "emblem" and a "holy sign" of what we have yet to see. Even in the New Testament, Father and Spirit remain hidden behind such holy signs as "voice" and "dove." The emblems and holy signs of the Old Testament, therefore, do not reveal the Holy Trinity as such, but are prophetic foreshadowings of the way in which the three divine persons make themselves accessible *now* to the faithful, and indeed only to them. What is depicted is, therefore, only—and that "in an image"—the economic Trinity; its being for us.

Moreover, we notice that between this being of God "in itself" and his being "for us" there can be no contradiction, for the true God reveals himself as none other than he really is. Theology, therefore, justly draws conclusions from the activity of God *ad extra*, revealed to us, about his being *ad intra*, hidden from our eye and mind. In the always common, even if personally distinct, saving activity of the Holy Trinity, which proceeds from the Father and reaches us through the Son in the Spirit, in order again to lead us in the Spirit through the Son to the Father, we may surely discern a *reflection* of the intra-Trinitarian life of God without being able to say anything about the how—let alone being able to depict it.

Old Testament events reappear in Christian iconography because of their typological meaning; that is, insofar as the Church is able to see in them a hidden reference to the fulness of revelation found in the New Testament. To these events belongs, too, as the theologian and hymnographer Metrophanes of Smyrna (ninth century) frequently recalls in his canon on the Trinity, the "hospitality of Abraham."

> Abraham, having become a sacred initiate, once received under holy signs, the Creator of all, and God and Lord, receiving them in three Persons with joy and recognizing the unique power of the three Persons.[8]

The icon of the Holy Trinity is therefore of rather a different kind than an icon of Christ. For Christ appeared to us "in the reality and the nature of flesh";[9] Abraham's three guests were, in contrast—in this comparable with the visions of the prophets Isaias and Daniel[10]—an "emblem" and "holy sign" of one God in three persons.

In a depiction of Gen 18, the mysterious, typological character of the Old Testament scene must not be destroyed, but can be only cautiously rendered open to the New Testament fulfilment of the "image." In particular, the identity of all three divine persons was certainly not revealed in the Old Testament. Only the Lord was

7 *Triodion*, Sunday of Orthodoxy, Great Vespers, sticheron 3.

8 *Paraklitiki*, Sunday, Canon of the Midnight Office, tone 8, ode 1, troparion 3; cf. also the texts already cited above: tone 1, ode 1, troparion 2; tone 3, ode 4, theotokion; tone 5, ode 8, troparion 1.

9 *Triodion*, Sunday of Orthodoxy, Lauds, sticheron 2.

10 *Paraklitiki*, Canon of the Midnight Office, tone 3, ode 5, troparion 1; tone 4, ode 6, troparion 2; tone 5, ode 4, troparion 1.

designated as person, as Christ, though in a concealed way. For a long time, it had been recognized that this Lord had been revealed to Abraham, veiled in the form of a man or an angel. Iconography took account of this, particularly in the christological type, where the central figure was made known as the Son by various attributes.

If Rublev wanted to show not only— as with some late-Byzantine icons of the Trinitarian type—the equality of essence, but also the individual characteristics of each of the three persons in the angels who symbolize them, while preserving the full typological character of the Old Testament scene, then the only possibility left to him was to give each of the two other figures "countenances" that could not be interchanged. If, in the figure of the Son, he could find support in the centuries-long tradition of the christological type, with the rendering of the Father and the Spirit he had to venture on to entirely new territory. That he achieved this highly risky characterization by the most delicate means perhaps points more than anything else to his artistic, and spiritual, maturity.

❧

Rublev depicts the three angels, as in many older icons of the Trinitarian type, as the same in form and size. All three carry the same staves in their hands, and sit on the same type of throne. They are the three divine persons, of equal essence, as Orthodox dogma has taught since the Second Ecumenical Synod (fourth century) and as has been sung in the liturgy since then.

> In equality of essence, I praise you, Thearchy, as equally glorified in the persons. For as life from life and giver of life, you exist ineffably. One is our God, and none is holy, save you, O Lord.[11]

> Mortal words are not sufficient to sing hymns to you, Unity without beginning. But as we are able, we dare to offer in faith glory and praise to your power, Triad, equally throned, beyond divinity.[12]

However, despite the same essence, there are individual distinctions in what characterizes personhood: posture, attitude, and gesture, that is, the personal characteristics of the three divine figures and their relationship to one another, which is likewise in correspondence with Orthodox teaching.

> Unapproachable Triad, co-eternal Thearchy without beginning, unchanging in everything save the radiant individual properties, abolish every wicked counsel of those who oppose us and the assault of the demons, and preserve me ever unharmed, Lord of all.[13]

> As we proclaim a single form of the Godhead in three personal and distinct individual properties, of the Father and the Son and the Spirit, we call out: praised are you, God of our fathers.[14]

> In the might of equal glory we praise the monarchic Thearchy in three persons, mutually unchanging, possessing a single distinction: the individual property of each existent.[15]

11 Ibid., tone 2, ode 3, troparion 1.

12 Ibid., tone 5, ode 9, troparion 1.

13 Ibid., tone 2, ode 8, troparion 1.

14 Ibid., tone 3, ode 7, troparion 2.

15 Ibid., tone 7, ode 6, troparion 1.

Each figure, then, is also clothed in the same types of garments—*chiton* and *himation*—which are individually distinct. This goes, too, for the characteristic tone of the garments, which works with a limited palate of colours: purple, pale green, and the one colour that is common to all three—an intense blue.

The meaning of the persons is finally expressed by drawing on those few elements from the old patterns that Rublev has taken and reduced to the role of pure symbols: the cubic altar table with a single vessel in the form of a chalice, together with, in the background, biblical reminiscences of a house, a tree, and a rock arranged in a single pattern.

In contrast, we can discount the geometrical figures, which lie behind the composition of the picture and to which immense significance has often been given. They tell us no more than we already know: the oneness of the essence and the threeness of the persons. They tell us nothing about the mutual relationships of the persons, save perhaps about the *monarchia* of the Father, which for the Trinitarian theology of the Eastern Church is particularly important. For in an equilateral triangle, inscribed in a circle, no corner is privileged.

Again, the arrangement of the composition is important. As we have previously mentioned, Rublev modifies the Trinitarian types in a striking way. In the christological icons, the central angel, through its frontal attitude and often its size as well, completely dominates the picture and reduces the two other angels to accompanying figures, whereas the Trinitarian icons to some extent breaks up this focus through the slight turning of the central angel. The central angel, though, still continues to look at the beholder.

Here, Rublev carefully breaks from tradition, even from his immediate predecessors at St Sergii Monastery. The central angel and the one on the right incline towards the one on the left and look towards it, while the one on the left looks towards the one on the right, giving the indication of relationship between the three persons. In this scheme, the angel on the left becomes the centre of the relationships within the whole composition. This is not a matter of chance but is a carefully calculated design. Here is the starting point for our interpretation.

If the three divine hypostases are perfectly equal in essence, and if they are considered living persons, and not just abstract principles, then there must hold sway among them an intra-Trinitarian hierarchy that is determined by the *monarchia* of the Father. This we know from the self-revelation of the Trinitarian God in saving history, not from rational speculation.

The source of the Godhead is, according to Orthodox understanding, not some essence lying behind the persons, but the person of the Father, who "dwells in unapproachable light" (1 Tim 6.16) and "whom no one can see" (Jn 1.18). The Father, so the Church teaches, is and has always been the Father of the Son and the principle of the Spirit, with no beginning point of origin, for God is not in space and time.

> As source and root, you are as Father the origin of the consubstantial
> Godhead in the Son and your Holy Spirit. So let therefore the three-

sunned light shine into my heart and enlighten it through participation in the deifying ray.[16]

As a double-crowned root, sprung from the Father as from a single root, so are the Son and the good Spirit, consubstantial branches derived from God, blossoms equally without beginning, as three lights of the Godhead.[17]

From the Father without beginning as from a root, there derive equally without beginning the Word and the Spirit, like branches of the Thearchy beyond being, revealing the single glory and power of the Trinity, which all we the faithful sing to the ages.[18]

Revealed to us is the "invisible" (Col 1.15), "the Father who abides in secret" (Matt 6.6), only through his Son, the only true exegete of the Father (Jn 1.18), and through the Spirit who comes to us from the Father through the Son (Jn 15.26).

As intellect is the unbegotten Father proclaimed to the wise in an image, as the Word, equally without beginning, the consubstantial Son and as the Holy Spirit the one who accomplished in the Virgin the Incarnation of the Son.[19]

The Word, begotten for an ineffable reason from the sun of the Father, rose as another eternal sun in the last days from the Virgin, teaching the unique, incomprehensible God in three persons.[20]

Son and Spirit always appear in saving history together, without confusion as to their persons. Therefore, they must stand within the Trinity in a unique, distinct, but mutually related, relationship to the Father. Orthodox theology consciously leaves open the how of this theological relationship, restricting itself to the biblical expression of the economic relationship. Only the being of the Son and the Spirit in saving history is therefore capable of depiction: *ad extra*, "for our sake." In an infinitely tender and yet compelling way, Andrei Rublev understood how to make this evident.

୬

The angel on the left is distinct from the other two both in attitude, gesture, and posture and also in the way his garments are worn and their colouring. He alone sits upright, while the other two incline towards him. He thus symbolizes the Father, from whom the Son and the Spirit go forth in their own ineffable way, but to whom they also lead the whole creation. The *chlamys* in pale purple, enhanced with gold (gold *assiste*), also points to the Father—who for us is still invisible—his form almost completely veiled, only allowing us to see very little of the radiant azure of his *chiton*. Finally, the house, rising immediately behind him, points to the Father, for "in my Father's house are many rooms" (Jn 14.2). The meaning of the posture and gesture of this angel, as well as that of the two other angels, will be explored in the following chapter.

୬

16 Ibid., tone 2, ode 1, troparion 2.

17 Ibid., tone 3, ode 4, troparion 1.

18 Ibid., tone 3, ode 8, troparion 1.

19 Ibid., tone 1, ode 1, theotokion.

20 Ibid., tone 7, ode 6, theotokion.

In christological icons, as well as in many Trinitarian icons, the figure in the centre is always wearing clothing characteristic both in form and colour, which designates him, quite apart from any other attributes, as Christ the Son. Over his body, he wears a dark purple *chiton*, often decorated with two—only one of which is visible—stripes (*clavus*) worked through with gold, while for an overgarment he has a *chlamys* of deep azure-blue, which is always worn so as to leave his right arm free. In this regard, Rublev keeps to tradition and practice. Those copyists, who from the fifteenth century onwards gave the central angel a cross nimbus inscribed with the words "He who is," and even an inscription IC XC, not only reflect the traditional interpretation, but also capture Rublev's intention (plate 23).

As in icons of Christ, the Incarnate One is depicted in his role in saving history as the "anointed of God," king and prophet in one. Hence, the costly purple and gold embroidered royal robe, which he wears on the body "which is given for you" (Lk 22.19), and the prophet's mantle. While the angel representing the "invisible Father" wears a heavenly azure-blue *chiton*, which is scarcely seen because it is almost entirely covered by a pale purple *chlamys*, the angel representing the Son wears it as the prevailing colour, alongside the dark purple. The Son has revealed to us, even in the flesh, his "glory," which he has as the "only-begotten of the Father"; his disciples have "seen" this (Jn 1.14) and "testify to it" (1 Jn 1.2). The self-offering of the Son is indicated by the figure on the right, who points to the chalice-like vessel containing the head of the sacrificed calf. The tree, too, emerging behind the Son, a symbol of the Tree of Life/the Wood of the Cross, points to this connexion.

⁂

It would seem to be most difficult to render the Holy Spirit, so as to make him clearly known, for his personal being has been revealed to us but not his countenance. We know his characteristics only through his connexion with the Father and the Son in the history of salvation and through his activity among us. Rublev, however, knew how to make known in a masterly way this humble reserve of the Spirit. Like the Son, the angel on the right, who symbolizes the Holy Spirit, also inclines towards the Father, from whom he proceeds according to the teaching of the Bible (Jn 15.26) and the Church (cf. the Creed of 381, without the *Filioque*). As with the Son, the *chlamys* is worn in such a way that leaves an arm free. In this case, it is the left arm, as opposed to the right arm of the angel representing the Son—an allusion to the primordial teaching of the Fathers (Irenaeus), according to which the Son and the Spirit are equally the two "hands" of the Father, through which he works everything.

As with the Son, the heavenly azure-blue of the *chiton* is clearly seen and reveals to us the Spirit, whom the Son sent to us from the Father as the "other Paraclete" (Jn 14.16; 15.26), as the Son himself revealed. His *chlamys* is pale-green, which, in Russia at least, is the liturgical colour of Pentecost, when churches are also lavishly decorated with branches of fresh greenery. Green is, therefore, a symbol of new life that the Spirit, the "Giver of Life," as he is called in the office of Pentecost, engenders and causes to grow. The ground on which all three figures find themselves is also pale-green.

СТАА ГЦА

IC XC

PLATE 23

Double-sided icon from the Cathedral of Sophia in Novgorod; end of fifteenth century; London.

Finally, behind the angel on the right a rock rises up, which can be understood as a symbol of earth, whose "face is renewed by the Spirit," as it says in the Vesper psalm of the Orthodox Church (Ps 103.30), and on which he will accomplish his work until the second *Parousia* of the Son. Some early copies of the icon show that the rock originally was cracked, which suggests another interpretation that would be still more appropriate to the context of the icon in the liturgy and saving history. It recalls the rock that was split by Moses' staff, causing living water to flow out for the thirsty people (Ex 17.6). The Apostle Paul already interpreted this "spiritual rock" as a symbol of Christ (1 Cor 10.4), but Christ himself interpreted the "streams of living water" as the Holy Spirit (Jn 7.38f.). It is worth noting that the Orthodox Church uses the text in John as a festal reading for Pentecost. According to this interpretation, the Son is symbolized by a rock, as well as a tree. In Rublev's icon the rock is situated behind the Spirit. Son and Spirit, who both come from the Father, always appear in saving history together and are related to each other in a unique fashion. It is the fulness of this mystery, however, as it is revealed to us at Pentecost, that we are now to see.

CHAPTER TEN

The Johannine Pentecost

Already more than a thousand years old by the time of Rublev, the theological and iconographic traditions of the Eastern Church do not provide a simple interpretation of the event in Gen 18. The theological depth of the fulness of the self-offering of God, given in Christ through the Holy Spirit, is set forth in the course of the centuries with different, yet mutually complementary emphases, with iconography developing its own means of making visible these ever new aspects. As the various iconographical types developed, with the help of artistically and spiritually gifted painters, they expressed ever more purely the underlying theological thoughts. In the fifteenth century, what new emphasis could theology set forth and a gifted icon-painter transpose into a picture, after the understanding of Gen 18 had already reached the completed fulness of a Trinitarian reading of the event?

As we have seen, the late-Byzantine period is determined by the struggle over the question of how God, unapproachable by creatures in his uncreated being, truly communicates himself, and how human beings can experience this self-communication in the mystical life. St Gregory Palamas responds thus: God communicates himself in his "divine and uncreated energies (or activities)," which are not the same as his uncreated "essence" and yet are God himself. These "energies," also called "grace," are the workings of the Holy Spirit; "their greatness cannot be told and they are numberless," as Palamas, together with Basil the Great, says,[1] "who illuminates and makes holy our souls" (Office of Pentecost).

Out of this fundamental insight, the Orthodox Church has developed a spirituality, which embraces the practice and teaching of a life wholly and completely under the guidance of the Holy Spirit. We see this reflected in this Pentecost text, which is said at the beginning of the daily offices:

> Heavenly King, Comforter, Spirit of Truth, everywhere present, filling all things, treasure of blessings and giver of life, come and abide in us, cleanse us from every stain, and, O Good One, save our souls.

The mirror of such a spiritual life is the life of St Sergii of Radonezh, in the light of whose radiance Rublev's *Troitsa* developed. Called by the Holy Spirit in his mother's womb and destined as a chosen vessel, the grace of the Holy Spirit took possession of him early on and filled him so greatly, that it was finally manifested in visible signs.

Father Pavel Florensky was not completely wrong when he maintained that St Sergii was, alongside Andrei Rublev, the true creator of the famed *Troitsa*.[2] One may even go a step further and suggest that this icon, painted in the "dwelling place of the Holy Trinity" built by Sergii, is intended to depict this mystery of the

1 Gregory Palamas, *Capita CL*, 68 (*Philokalia* IV, London 1995, p. 377).

2 Florensky, *The Trinity–St Sergius Lavra and Russia*, p. 25; *Iconostasis*, p. 84.

grace of the Holy Spirit. From this milieu sprang an icon of the Holy Trinity with attributes never seen before, influenced by the theology of the Pentecostal feast. The attributes that Rublev used to make visible his inspiration are the postures and gestures of the three angels, to which we now want to turn.

&

At the centre of the whole composition, a vessel—paten and chalice in one—stands on an otherwise empty altar and in the vessel appears the head of a calf. Is the whole composition a symbol of a heavenly liturgy, origin and model of the earthly liturgy?[3] Yes and no. From the point of view of the beholder, the Son sits behind the altar, or so it seems to the unbiased eye. Still, we are dealing with a liturgical scenario—of that the altar and the chalice leave us in no doubt—whose content has yet to be determined more precisely, for the perspective is clearly not that of the painter. The right-angled opening in the altar clearly gives one to understand that this is the east side, turned away from the people. But that means that the Father and the Spirit sit behind the altar; Christ, however, the high priest is in front the altar, which is turned to face east, like the earthly priest at the offering of the unbloody sacrifice. As with many, even Western, liturgical depictions, we are, therefore, dealing with a reversal of perspective. The picture secures for the beholder an insight into an event that is not accessible to his direct sight.

Let us now look at the posture and gesture of the three angels. The Son bows towards the Father and looks at him. His right hand seems to point at the chalice; yet, at the same time, beyond it towards the Spirit. It is evident that this is part of the design of the painter because the right hand of the Son was originally closed and only the index finger pointed over the chalice to the Spirit, which became clear in the restoration of the icon. This peculiar position of the finger must have seemed incomprehensible to the first copyists of the fifteenth century because they added the middle finger to the index finger. In this sense, even the original has been touched up. Sadly, the restorers at the beginning of the twentieth century did not undo this early retouching and significantly changed the sense of the gesture by making it one of blessing instead of referring.[4]

This apparently trifling detail—the Son's gesture of pointing to the Spirit—makes clear that the attention of the painter is directed at the Spirit, in contrast to the pattern of composition that shows the Son, traditionally, as the focal point. The Father's posture and gesture confirm this, for the Father, apparently, returns neither the gaze nor the gesture of the Son, but looks at the Spirit, to whom his right hand, raised in blessing, is directed. The Spirit, finally, bows his head humbly before the Father, and his right hand, lowered towards the table, seems to want to underline this movement.

&

If one compares Rublev's original with one of the numerous early copies, it becomes clear how peculiar and difficult it was to establish the hidden reality perceivable to the senses. The biggest problem that confronted the copyists seems to have been how to render the gestures. We have already referred to the retouching of the Son's right hand; this earlier retouching is found, in my view, in all the older

3 This relationship has been most often maintained in modern times. It has ancient roots, as we have already seen. See pp. 27–29 on S. Vitale and S. Maria Maggiore. Cf. also the fresco of the Holy Trinity (1176–1185/90) on the east wall of the little Chapel of the Mother of God in the Monastery of St John on Patmos, where it is found exactly above the altar (Papadopoulos, *Monastery of St John*, figures 5 and 6). In more recent times, it is represented on a ciborium of the same monastery (eighteenth century). In the uppermost of the three areas, the "Philoxenia of Abraham" (so the Greek title) appears, below and on a larger scale the "Mystical Supper," that is, Christ with his disciples at the supper table (Papadopoulos, *Monastery of St John*, figure 22). The same thought lies behind a small Russian icon (private collection), on which, in the nimbus of each of the three angels, the word "holy" is inscribed—a reference to the Thrice-holy of the Divine Liturgy. The examples could be increased at will.

4 Cf. Müller, *Dreifaltigkeitsikone*, p. 66f., who, however, on the basis of another identification of the three angels (from left to right: Spirit–Father–Son) comes to a completely different interpretation of this gesture.

copies. When considering also the gestures of the angels on the left and on the right, the copyists clearly did not know how to begin. Thus, two further chalices are almost always added—from the more ancient models—in order to establish a relationship. The monk Paissii (1484–85) even renders the angel on the right as grasping a piece of—again introduced—bread. These, and other assimilations to convention, show that Rublev's personal message was clearly not understood.

&

If the postures and gestures are taken in the way that Rublev meant, then a movement becomes visible between the three figures, which makes evident a wordless conversation between Father, Son, and Holy Spirit. What could the content of this intra-divine conversation be? The chalice in the middle of the altar table and, in it, the head of the calf seem to suggest the conclusion that here we become witnesses of the eternal decision of the Father to send the Son with the help of the Spirit for the redemption of humankind. Yet, this interpretation of the situation does not do justice to the fact that the postures and gestures of this intra-divine conversation do not point toward the Son, but rather at the Spirit, to whom the Father and the Son refer in their own ways.

The Holy Spirit first emerges from the shadows—equal to the Father and the Son and sent by them—at Pentecost, becoming at that point in time an actor in the history of salvation: Pentecost, moreover, as described by that beloved disciple who at the Last Supper was the only one allowed to rest on the breast of the Lord. Rublev's *Troitsa*, the theological context of which is Pentecost, can be "read" as a depiction in colour and shape of the Johannine account of Jesus' Farewell Discourse, which is completely shot through with the mystery, now being revealed, of the Triune God.

The very first sentences point to the goal of the saving action of God in his Son: the house of the Father.

> "Let not your hearts be troubled; believe in God, believe also in me. In my Father's house are many rooms; if it were not so, would I have told you that I go to prepare a place for you? And when I go and prepare a place for you, I will come again and will take you to myself, that where I am you may be also." (Jn 14.1–3)

The way to the house of the Father is the Son himself (Jn 14.4–7). Yet, the Son is going back to the Father, from whom he set out. Will his disciples, therefore, be left behind as "orphans" (Jn 14.18f.)?

> "If you love me, you will keep my commandments. And I will pray the Father, and he will give you another Counsellor, to be with you for ever, even the Spirit of truth, whom the world cannot receive, because it neither sees him nor knows him; you know him, for he dwells with you, and will be in you." (Jn 14.15–17)

The task of this Paraclete who will remain until the second Parousia of the Son is first of all to witness to the Son.

> "But when the Counsellor comes, whom I shall send to you from the Father, even the Spirit of truth, who proceeds from the Father, he will bear witness of me." (Jn 15.26)

Yet, the disciples, too, whom Christ sends into the world, as he himself was sent by the Father (Jn 20.21), are to be witnesses (Jn 15.27). The Paraclete is the one who makes such witness possible.

> "I have yet many things to say to you, but you cannot bear them now. When the Spirit of truth comes, he will guide you into all the truth; for he will not speak on his own authority, but whatever he hears he will speak, and he will declare to you the things that are to come. He will glorify me, for he will take what is mine and declare it to you." (Jn 16.12–14)

Finally, the Son reveals, in his prayer of departure to the Father, why he became human: to introduce those who believe in him to that unfathomable communion that he has with his Father.

> When Jesus had spoken these words, he lifted up his eyes to heaven and said, "Father, the hour has come; glorify thy Son that the Son may glorify thee, since thou hast given him power over all flesh, to give eternal life to all whom thou hast given him. And this is eternal life, that they know thee the only true God, and Jesus Christ whom thou hast sent. I glorified thee on earth, having accomplished the work which thou gavest me to do; and now, Father, glorify thou me in thy own presence with the glory which I had with thee before the world was. . . . The glory which thou has given me I have given to them, that they may be one even as we are one, I in them and thou in me, that they may become perfectly one, so that the world may know that thou hast sent them and hast loved them even as thou has loved me. Father, I desire that they also, whom thou has given me, may be with me where I am, to behold thy glory which thou hast given me, for thou didst love me before the foundation of the world." (Jn 17.1–3, 22–24)

Between this promise and its fulfilment stands the Cross and afterwards the Resurrection, the glorification of the Son, through which is the Spirit set free (Jn 7.39).

> So they took Jesus, and he went out, bearing his own cross, to the place called the place of a skull, which is called in Hebrew Golgotha. There they crucified him, and with him two others, one on either side, and Jesus between them. . . . When Jesus had received the vinegar, he said, "It is finished"; and he bowed his head and gave up his spirit. . . . But one of the soldiers pierced his side with a spear, and at once there came out blood and water. He who saw it has borne witness—his testimony is true, and he knows that he tells the truth—that you also may believe. (Jn 19.17–18, 30–34)

After Christ has left his own for a little while, he comes to them again on Easter morning, to fulfil his promise.

On the evening of that day, the first day of the week, the doors being shut where the disciples were, for fear of the Jews, Jesus came and stood among them and said to them, "Peace be with you." When he had said this, he showed them his hands and his side. Then the disciples were glad when they saw the Lord. Jesus said to them again, "Peace be with you. As the Father has sent me, even so I send you." And when he had said this, he breathed on them, and said to them, "Receive the Holy Spirit. If you forgive the sins of any, they are forgiven; if you retain the sins of any, they are retained." (Jn 20.19–23)

In an infinitely tender way, Andrei Rublev understood how to make this Johannine Pentecost manifest. The movement between the three divine persons, the intra-Trinitarian conversation, proceeds from the Son: With entreaty he looks at the Father, while his right hand points to the chalice of his Passion and beyond that to the Spirit. This look and this gesture intimate the request for the sending of the Paraclete, which only becomes possible through the self-sacrifice of the Son. The Father, who always hears the Son (Jn 11.42), fulfils this request: His gaze is directed to the Spirit, who is enthroned with him behind the altar table, and his right hand bestows on him the blessing for this completion of the saving work of the Son. The Holy Spirit, however, bows his head in humble assent, which is shown by his lowered right hand. Behind the Paraclete, the rock—probably represented as cracked by Rublev—suggests in a symbol that the live-giving streams of the Holy Spirit pour forth from the opened side of the mystical rock, that is, Christ.

❧

It seems, then, that this is the particular emphasis that Rublev wanted to set forth in his *Troitsa*, which certainly does not exclude other, already well-known interpretations, but to some extent even includes them, yet in its way is unique. It is the sending of the person of the Holy Spirit, who came from the Father through the Son and owing to the self-sacrifice of the Son, which we commemorate at Pentecost, as John has alone described for us.

For while the traditional icon of Pentecost depicts the Apostles "clothed with power from on high" (Lk 24.49, cf. Acts 1.8) through the outpouring of the Holy Spirit—symbolized in the tongues of fire (Acts 2.1–4)—which unexpectedly made inspired prophets and evangelists out of simple Galilaean fishermen, it is only made clear in the Farewell Discourses of the Fourth Gospel that this Holy Spirit is not only God's power, but also the mysterious third person of the Holy Trinity. He is that abiding Spirit, who so completely proceeds in the Son, without being mixed up with him as person, that Christ can designate him as the "other Paraclete,"[5] whom in his stead he requests and obtains for us from the Father. This mystery of the personal being of the Spirit, moreover, is only made visible in that icon that for a long time has symbolized the Holy Trinity.

Rublev's brilliant achievement, therefore, consists in having created an icon, which for the first time not only depicts the three divine hypostases, but also manifests each of them in their unchangeable uniqueness as persons, that is, in their relationship to the other persons, insofar as this is known in their individual activity in the history of salvation: going out from the Father, through the Son in the

5 In the German original, the title of the book was *Der andere Paraklet*, that is, "the other Paraclete," to which reference is made here—Trans.

Holy Spirit—and again in the Spirit returning to the Father through the Son. Florensky had already grasped this intuitively when he designated Rublev as the real creator of an icon of the Holy Trinity,[6] even though there had been icons of the hospitality of Abraham, which bear this title, for more than five hundred years.

❧

This new emphasis that Rublev wanted to set forth can appropriately be called "pneumatic-spiritual." For if the earliest Christian interpretation of Gen 18 is accentuated in a christological-soteriological way, insofar as it finds in the manifestation of God before Abraham a hidden foreshadowing of the Incarnation of Jesus Christ the Redeemer, so the later development of the classical Trinitarian-theological interpretation sees in the three visitors a type of the three hypostases of the one essence of God.

With Rublev, the emphasis shifts away from these interpretations—while taking up everything that tradition had previously produced—to the participation by grace of the creature in the personal being of the Holy Trinity, something that first becomes a reality at Pentecost. This, however, resulted in the Byzantine tradition in nothing else than the personal indwelling of the Holy Spirit.

Rublev does not seem to stand alone with regard to this mystical intuition. In a manuscript of the Liturgy of St John Chrysostom, decorated with miniatures, the picture of the Holy Trinity serves to illustrate precisely[7] the words spoken by the priest after the epiclesis:

> So that those who partake of them [that is, the gifts of bread and wine changed by the descent of the Holy Spirit into the body and blood of Christ] may obtain vigilance of soul, forgiveness of sins, communion of your Holy Spirit, fulness of the Kingdom of heaven, freedom to speak in your presence, not judgment or condemnation.[8]

In his way and in the particular context of the Divine Liturgy, the painter of this miniature clearly wanted to express the same idea that Rublev made visible by other means. This particular emphasis can be called "pneumatic," insofar as within the mystery of the Trinity it particularly has the Holy Spirit in view, but "spiritual," insofar as, thanks to this personal gift and indwelling of the Spirit, there develops what we call the spiritual life.

With this Johannine Pentecost, as Rublev has depicted it, there begins quite genuinely what we call Christian existence: rebirth in the Holy Spirit (Jn 3); new life in the light of the Spirit of truth, which finds its highest expression here on earth in that "worship of the Father in spirit and truth" (Jn 4.23), that is, "in the Holy Spirit and in the Only-begotten Son" (Evagrios Pontikos), and is a foretaste of that heavenly fulfilment of being one in God that Christ has promised. This new life is, in the true sense of the word, a "spiritual life," that is, a life lived completely and wholly from the fulness of the grace of the Paraclete, which takes over the "guiding" (cf. Jn 16.13)—an example of such a life as led in archetypal fashion by St Sergii of Radonezh, whom God so transformed that, even on earth, he became a "new man," a "chosen vessel of the Holy Spirit," the "dwelling-place and servant of the Holy Trinity."

6 Florensky, *Iconostasis*, p. 84.

7 The three angels together form the first letter (omega) of the first word of the *epiklesis*.

8 Cf. Grabar, "Un rouleau liturgique constantinopolitain," p. 175, plate 15. H.-J. Schultz (*Byzantine Liturgy*, p. 86) relates our miniature to the persons of the Most Holy Trinity in general as the "ultimate recipients of the sacrifice and the primary givers of the graces won by the sacrifice." If one sticks to the wording, then it is indeed only a matter of those gifts of grace, in which we partake through communion in the Holy Mysteries. Among these, the "communion in the Holy Spirit" refers immediately to the Holy Trinity, and it may be this that caused the artist to place their picture here. For only through the mediation of the Holy Spirit, and thanks to the sacrifice of the Son, do we gain access to the Father, to whom the prayer is directed.

Thus, the icon of the Holy Trinity became more than just one of the numerous festal icons that are displayed only on a particular day in the Church's year and set up for the veneration of the faithful. Pentecost, the feast of the abiding Paraclete, is every day. The Orthodox Church has always been genuinely conscious of this; the texts particularly characteristic of Pentecost are repeated, as we have seen, at every office and each Divine Liturgy. The goal of human life is, indeed, to quote once again St Seraphim of Sarov, the "acquisition of the Holy Spirit," of the "general grace of the Holy Trinity."[9]

Where else than in the spiritually radiant realm of St Sergii of Radonezh could another saint, Andrei Rublev, have painted his incomparable *Troitsa*? Yet again the priest and martyr Pavel Florensky was right when he ventured this unusual "proof of the existence of God": "There exists the icon of the Trinity by St Andrei Rublev; therefore, God exists."[10]

9 Florensky, *The Trinity–St Sergius Lavra and Russia*, p. 17.

10 Florensky, *Iconostasis*, p. 68.

CHAPTER ELEVEN

The Vision of God in Image and Likeness

According to its essence, the icon is not a private devotional picture, especially in the case of a major icon expressing a mystery of faith central to revelation. Rather, its theological place is the liturgy, where it complements the proclamation of the word with the proclamation of the image. Therefore, if we want to grasp the message of such an icon, we must, as with the preaching of the Church in general, start neither from essentially foreign preconceptions nor from merely subjective impressions. We must, rather, let ourselves be guided by the unfolding of revelation in the teaching of the Church and its authentic expression as found in theology, liturgy, spirituality, and iconography. Brought to the way of the Father by this humble listening to Tradition, we may venture to surrender ourselves to our personal vision of the divine mysteries. This vision is a continuing event, the rhythm of which is determined by our own spiritual growth. In this life, we shall never reach any definitive end.

Even this personal vision is a matter of following in the steps of the Fathers. Joseph of Volokalamsk knew this when he reported from reliable sources that Daniil and Andrei Rublev, free from earthly cares, "continually raised their spirit and thoughts on high to the immaterial and divine light, but their physical eyes were always lifted up to the pictures painted in material colours of the Lord, his all-pure Mother and all the Saints . . . Therefore they sat on chairs, even on the feast day of the radiant Resurrection of Christ, in front of the divine and all-pure icons and looked at them uninterruptedly, and were thus filled with divine joy and radiance. And not only on this day did they do this, but also on other days, when they were not occupied with painting icons."

❧

Meditation on Andrei Rublev's Trinity

Pentecost. Fulness of the self-revelation of the Triune God.[1]

Outpouring of the Holy Spirit. No longer simply "power from on high" (Lk 1.35), but that "other," "abiding Paraclete," whom the Son has promised in his stead. The third person of the All-holy Trinity.

The gaze of contemplation rests on the festal icon of the painter-monk, St Andrei Rublev.

Three angels round a table. In the middle of them only a single chalice. In the background, a house, a tree, and a rock.

1 The following theological meditation on Rublev's Trinity recounts doctrinal points that have been presented more fully in the preceding text. Each reflection springs from the deep mystery of the revelation of Jesus Christ, made known by the will of the Father and the power of the Holy Spirit—Ed.

Of the biblical "hospitality of Abraham" only the head of the calf in the chalice is recalled. The hosts themselves, Abraham and Sarah, are missing.

Their place is taken by us, the faithful, among whom the Holy Trinity set up their tent.

The biblical event, recounted with such a delight for detail in Gen 18, is compressed to the furthest limit. No historical narrative tale.

The divine light of fulfilment has completely swallowed up the Old Testament type, the preliminary sketch and likeness.

Transparence of the earthly, the creaturely, to the divine reality. Primordial event as an image of timeless presence.

❧

The beholding eye wanders from one to another. Beginning with the "abiding Paraclete," that is, indeed Pentecost, the eye wanders further to the unique true "exegete" of the Father, of whom the Spirit bears witness, that is, the Son, who alone rests *in sinu Patris*—in the Father's bosom—and allows itself to be led from him to the Father, whom without the Son no one has ever seen, and to whom no one comes, save through the Son.

Full of awe, the gaze remains with the Father without beginning, and sinks into the mystery of his *monarchia*, the source of all being: of the Son and the Spirit in a manner equally without beginning, each in its own, non-interchangeable way, through "begetting" and through "proceeding."

The source, too, of everything created, by grace eternally present in the Son and the Spirit, yet not without beginning as they are, for their creation has a beginning.

For there never was a time when the Father was not the Father of the Son and the source of the Spirit. He *is* Father; he does not *become* Father.

Not only are the Son and the Spirit from the Father, but they are also to him, which is indicated through the tender inclination of the angels in the centre and on the right to the one on the left.

The gaze embraces the three divine persons: the source and goal, too, of all created being. Coming forth from the heart of the Father, from the fount of the life-giving Trinity.

Having become, in the Spirit, the adopted son of the Father, the beholder ventures a shy look at the ultimate source of his own being. Since, in a mysterious way, he has his roots in the unfathomable mystery of the three divine persons without beginning. Spoken from the Father in the Spirit as an adjective of the Word.

Inexhaustible fulness of life, so overflowing, that it can itself create a space for being that, even though not equal in being, yet has a share in its fulness of being through grace to which we have no right.

Who could comprehend created being without the revelation of the uncreated being of God, who in three persons is essentially one? Being that has a beginning but no end through participation in that which is without end?

❧

Thought advances further to the way, both tragic and beautiful, that this created being has taken. His fashioning by the two "hands" of the Father, according to the image of God (Gen 1.27), that is, by the Son and the Spirit, equally as an image of an image. His determination one day, too, to become like him (1 Jn 3.2, cf. Gen 1.26).

Yet, instead of being like God (Gen 3), first of all the Fall, of which he is himself guilty. Expulsion from the face of God. Hardship and suffering and finally the wages of sin: death (Rom 6.23).

Yet, as God had the first word, so to him alone belongs the last word.

The Son, the perfect image of the invisible God (Col 1.15), makes himself in the Spirit the way, goes after the fallen image throughout the ages, first in a hidden way, then he becomes human from the Virgin Mary. Goes after him even in his deepest humiliation: death, the death on a cross.

He descends into the realm of death; he breaks open the gates of the underworld; he rises in the brilliance of Easter morning to eternal life and becomes, for all who believe in him, the "pioneer of salvation" (Heb 2.10).

All this is succinctly indicated in the one chalice in the middle of the altar, in the Tree of Life—the Wood of the Cross.

The gaze remains fixed on this chalice: the central point of the icon and the axis of a wordless intra-divine conversation, indicated in the gaze and gesture of the three angels. My being, my salvation, as the subject of conversation between Father, Son, and Spirit.

Thought plunges still more deeply into the unfathomable mystery; it attempts to grasp the "how" of salvation: the "kenosis" of the Son, indicated in the tree of the Cross and the chalice of the Passion, the "unblemished self-offering through the eternal Spirit" (Heb 9.14), the completion of the self-emptying of the Incarnation wrought by the Spirit.

And then the fruit of this kenosis is indeed Pentecost: the setting free of the Holy Spirit from the open side of the glorified Son (Jn 7.39, 19.34), of the "rock."

❧

It now remains to direct our gaze to the Spirit. He follows the right hand of the Son, which points to the chalice of the Passion, the accomplished sacrifice, and at the same time beyond that to the Spirit. Then his eye follows the gaze of the Son, which is directed to the Father in entreaty: "I will pray the Father, and he will give you another Counsellor. . . . " Contemplating the sublime form of the Father, wrapped in his light purple garment, shot through with gold, our gaze follows the gaze of the eye that is directed towards the Spirit, and his right hand, both blessing and pointing, which indicates the fulfilment of the Son's entreaty.

Again, turning to the eye of the figure on the right, the "Spirit of truth," which will "guide us into all the truth," in all those things, that we cannot bear now.

The humble withdrawal of this other Paraclete behind the Son, to whom he will bear witness and whom he will glorify, and whose words he will bring to our remembrance, fills the heart with amazement: the utmost kenosis! The all-presence and yet incomprehensibility of being as person.

Thought plunges still deeper in meditation on the activity of this Paraclete abiding with us: his teaching (Jn 14.26), his prophetic "declaring the things that are to come" (Jn 16.13), but also his incorruptible "conviction of the world in respect of sin and of righteousness and of judgment" (Jn 16.8). Truly another Paraclete, who, as simply our advocate with the Father, Jesus Christ (1 Jn 2.1), does not speak or act on his own, but only "speaks what he hears" (Jn 16.13). For as the Son "has made known all that he has heard from the Father" (Jn 15.15), so, too, will the Spirit take what is the Son's and declare it to us (Jn 16.14), but that means finally again from the Father, for "all that the Father has is mine," that is, the Son's (Jn 16.15). So, that in everything that the Spirit will do and say, the Father and the Son are continually present in a hidden way: undivided Trinity.

Then, the eye removes a little distance and embraces with its gaze the whole picture: three angels around a table, and on it a chalice; house, tree, and rock, which tell of the visit of the "lords" to Abraham, the friend of God (Jas 2.23). Amazed, thought plunges into the mystery of image and reality, of the Old Testament promise and the New Testament fulfilment.

For had God not already announced in advance the future salvation of "our father Abraham?" So, "Abraham rejoiced that he was to see my day; he saw it and was glad" (Jn 8.56). He, indeed, foresaw that, "apart from us," to whom finally the promise has been granted, he "should not be made perfect" (Heb 11.40).

❧

And yet again the gaze embraces the whole picture: three figures united at a mystical meal around a table. Thought plunges into the mystery of the Divine Liturgy, its heavenly archetype and its earthly reflection. It beholds in spirit the "high priest after the order of Melchisedec," who, not with the blood of others, but with his own blood, advanced "through the veil of his flesh" into the presence of the Father to work reconciliation for us (Heb 10). Holy terror seizes the beholder at the thought that the Son's saving act through the power of the Holy Spirit becomes a continually new presence, shared with all the faithful, so that the "last" stand there no poorer than the "first." "We have seen the true light, we have received the heavenly Spirit. . . ."

❧

". . . another Paraclete, *that he may abide with you for ever*" (John 14.16). Since Easter it has been an ever-enduring Pentecost. Whoever has received the Holy Spirit (Jn 20.22), who proceeds from the Father, from the breath of the Risen One is a temple of the Holy Spirit (1 Cor 6.19), a dwelling place of the undivided Trinity. He is, in the true sense of the word, a "pneumatikos" (1 Cor 3.15f.), whose spiritual life is hidden with Christ in God (Col 3.3).

On the Origin of the Pilgrim Souvenir from Mambre

The following observations, offered by M. English Frazer, tell against a genuinely Christian, or even Christian-syncretistic, origin for the Pilgrim Souvenir from Mambre.

The three young men were according to the inscription (see the bottom of this page) understood as "angels." The three star-shaped loaves on the table suggest that they have some link to an astral cult. Added to that there is the depiction on the other side of the seal. A bejewelled goddess in a garment decorated with stars is enthroned between four (palm?) trees. The inscription designates her likewise as "heavenly." Elements clearly Jewish or Christian are completely absent.

On the historical background

Eusebios reports in his *Vita Constantini* III.52—and Sozomen, *Church History* II.4, takes it up later—that in Mambre, every year in summer, a much-frequented festival with a market was celebrated by Jews, pagans, and Christians. Each group gave an interpretation to the feast—quite syncretistically—in its own way. The Jews commemorated their descent from Abraham, the pagans the visit of the angels, the Christians the manifestation of the Son of God before Abraham—in the figure of one of the three men, among whom the Lord hid himself.

Constantine's stepmother, Eutropia, on the occasion of a visit to Mambre, took great offence at this openly peaceful mutual encounter of religions and made the emperor intervene. Constantine had the altar at Mambre destroyed and the wooden idols that were also there burnt to ashes. A church was built there, and the libations and sacrifices came to an end. In these pagan libations and sacrifices, the well of Abraham clearly played a special role: during the festivities wine, cakes, gold pieces, perfume, and incense were thrown in so that the water became undrinkable. Constantine forbade these ancient rites and threatened anyone who continued to celebrate them with severest punishment. This makes a dating of the pilgrim souvenirs to the fifth century rather improbable; they must be somewhat older.

Both inscriptions speak against a Christian origin of the double-sided seal. On the side depicting the three young men, we read: "May the angels be merciful to me," instead of an appeal to the Son of God, whom the Christians ostensibly venerated at Mambre. It is expressly mentioned by Eusebios (and Sozomen) that the pagans called upon the angels. The inscription on the other side, which depicts the goddess Aphrodite (or Isis, Astarte, or Atergatis), reads: "With joy I receive the heavenly."

The conclusion would seem to be that we are dealing with a pagan syncretism that possibly took over local, Jewish traditions about Abraham. The seal may very well have served to make those sacrificial cakes that the pagans threw into Abraham's well. That would account for the depiction of the three angels, but any Christian interpretation of Gen 18 is missing, which in this context is not to be looked for.

The star-motif on both sides of the seal suggests a pagan(-syncretistic) astral cult, and that the three young men and the "heavenly" woman are reflections of the cult-images venerated at Mambre. Were these those "idols" that Constantine later had burnt?

In another work (*The Proof of the Gospel,* V. 9.7), Eusebios again speaks of Mambre as a place that "even today is venerated as holy by those who live nearby to the glory of those who appeared to Abraham." At that time, there was still standing the terebinth of the manifestation. There was, too, a picture (*graphē*) depicting the three visitors. Eusebios does not state if the picture mentioned, of Christian origin, was only venerated by Christians. A direct relationship between the seal and the earliest, clearly Christian depictions of Gen 18 cannot be established. There are elements in the first depiction, such as the well and the birdcage, unknown to the later tradition, which moves entirely in the realm of the biblical account. Indirectly, there might appear to be a connexion, for instance, in the witness to Eusebios, picked up again by John of Damascus (see pp. 52f.).

Illustrations

Plate 1
Double-sided seal in limestone, diameter 14 cm; supposedly found near Jerusalem; fifth century (?). Metropolitan Museum of Art, New York. Cf. M. English Frazer, "Syncretistic Pilgrim's Mould."

Plate 2
Fresco from the catacomb on the Via Latina, Rome; cubiculum B, 96 x 94 cm; beginning of fourth century. Cf. Ferrua, *Unknown Catacomb*, p. 77, fig. 49; Stützer, *Kunst der römischen Katakomben*, p. 128; Fink, *Bildfrömmigkeit*.

Plate 3
Mosaic from Santa Maria Maggiore, Rome; nave, left side; first half of fifth century. Cf. Santini, *Santa Maria Maggiore*, p. 21.

Plate 4
Mosaic from San Vitale, Ravenna; sanctuary; middle of sixth century. Cf. Grabar, *La peinture byzantine*, p. 58; Marabini, *I mosaici di Ravenna*, pp. 50 and 51.

Plate 5
Mosaic from the Cappella Palatina, Palermo; between 1154 and 1166. Cf. Giordano, *Hofkapelle im Normannenpalast*.

Plate 6
Mosaic from the cathedral of Monreale; end of twelfth/beginning of thirteenth century. Cf. Chierichetti, *Dom von Monreale*, p. 58.

Plate 7
Mosaic from the cathedral of San Marco, Venice; part of the great Abraham cycle (second cupola of the narthex and lunettes); beginning of the thirteenth century. Cf. Bertoli, *I mosaici di San Marco*, Milan 1986, p. 110.

Plate 8
Miniature from a Greek Psalter; Bibliotheca Apostolica Vaticana, cod. Barb. gr. 372, p. 85; about 1092. Photo: Biblioteca Vaticana.

Plate 9
South "Golden Door" of the Church of the Nativity of the Mother of God, Suzdal; 31 x 23 cm; about 1230.

Plate 10
Feofan Grek, fresco from the Chapel of the Holy Trinity in the Church of the Transfiguration of Christ, Novgorod; 1378.

Plate 11
Quarter of a four-part icon (from left to right: Resurrection of Lazarus, Trinity, Jesus in the Temple, the Evangelist John with Prochoros) from the Church of St George in Novgorod; 43.5 x 33.7 cm.; first half of fifteenth century; Russian Museum, St Petersburg. Cf. Neubauer, *Kunst und Literatur,* p. 126.

Plate 12
Fresco from the cave church of Carikli Kilise, in Göreme, Anatolia; thirteenth century (?). Cf. Spitzing, *Lexikon byzantinisch,* coloured plate 10, and p. 273.

Plate 13
Icon from the Catholicon of Vatopedi, Athos; 117 x 92 cm; end of fourteenth century. Cf. Grabar, *Les revêtements en or et en argent des icons* , plate D.

Plate 14
Byzantine icon, part of an iconostasis; 33 x 60 cm; end of the fourteenth century; Benaki Museum, Athens. Cf. Grabar, *La peinture byzantine,* p. 192; Weitzmann, *The Icon,* p. 131, plate 46; Chatzidakis, *Benaki Museum* , p. 14 and fig. 23.

Plate 15
Greek icon; 15 x 31.3 cm; sixteenth century; Historical Museum, Moscow. Cf. Kyslassowa, *Russische Ikonen,* fig. 106.

Plate 16
Russian icon from the Trinity-St Sergii Lavra; 161 x 122 cm; beginning of the fifteenth century (about 1411?); Museum Sergiev Posad (formerly, Zagorsk). Cf. Smirnowa, fig. 62, description: pp. 270f.

Plate 17
So-called Zyrian Trinity, from the Church of the Trinity in the parish of Vozhemsk in Yarensk; 117 x 95 cm; end of fourteenth century; District Museum of Vologda.

Plate 18
Russian icon from Pskov; 145 x 108 cm; end of fifteenth/beginning of sixteenth century; Tretiakov Gallery, Moscow.

Plate 19
Double portrait of Emperor John VI Kantakouzenos (1347–1354), from a collection of his theological treatises; fourteenth century; Paris, Bibliothèque Nationale, grec 1242, fol. 123 v. Cf. Grabar, *La peinture byzantine,* p. 184.

Plate 20
Icon from the Cathedral of the Dormition in the Monastery of St Joseph of Volokalamsk; Monk Paissii; 151 x 120 cm; 1484/5; Museum Andrei Rublev, Moscow.

Plate 21
Icon from the Church of the Trinity of the Makhrishchskii Monastery; 141 x 111.5 cm; Historical Museum, Moscow. Cf. Kyslassowa, *Russische Ikonen,* fig. 45 (details:

46–47); first half of sixteenth century. According to Lebedewa, *Andrej Rubljow*, p. 124: 1430s or 1440s.

Plate 22
Copy of the original, completed in 1598 at the command of Tsar Boris Godunov; 146 x 116 cm; iconostasis of the Church of the Trinity in the Trinity-St Sergii Lavra, Sergiev Posad.

Plate 23
Double-sided icon from the Cathedral of Sophia in Novgorod; 24 x 19.5 cm; end of fifteenth century; London.

⁂

For the assembling of all the iconographic materials I am indebted to Betty Ambiveri of the Centro di documentazione della Biblioteca, Seriate, Italy, who also took responsibility for acquiring corresponding rights of the original German publication. My sincere thanks to Betty and the institute for this valuable service. —G.B.

Select Bibliography

[NOTE: The translator has supplemented this bibliography with English translations of works Bunge refers to in the original or in German translations. Titles of Russian works are given in English adding: (in Russian). Sources Bunge used for the liturgical hymns have been deleted, and instead reference is made directly to the service books, from which the translator has made his own fresh translations, save where the translation is otherwise attributed.]

Alpatov, M., "La 'Trinité' dans l'art byzantin et l'icone de Roublev," *Echos d'Orient* 30, 146 (1927), pp. 150–86.

Bertoli, B., *I mosaici di San Marco*, Milan 1986.

Bushkovitch, P., "The Limits of Hesychasm: Some Notes on Monastic Spirituality in Russia 1350–1500," *Forschungen zur osteuropäischen Geschichte* 38 (1986), pp. 97–109.

Chatzidakis, M., *Die griechischen Museen. Benaki Museum*. Athens 1978.

Chierichetti, S., *Der Dom von Monreale*, ed. 8, Palermo 1985.

Dëmina, N. A., *Andrei Rublev and the Painters of His Circle* (in Russian), Moscow 1972.

Eckhardt, Th., "Die Dreifaltigkeitsikone Rublevs und die russische Kunstwissenschaft," *Jahrbuch für Gechichte Osteuropas*, nf 6 (1958), pp. 145–76.

Engemann, J., "Zu den Dreifaltigkeitsdarstellungen der frühchristlichen Kunst. Gab es im 4 Jh. anthropomorphe Trinitätsbilder?" *Jahrbuch für Antike und Christentum* 19 (1976), pp. 157–72.

English Frazer, M., "The Syncretistic Pilgrim's Mould from Mambre (?)," *Gesta* 18 (1979), pp. 137–45.

_____, "Mold with the Three Angels at Mambre," in Weitzmann, *Age of Spirituality*, item 522 of the catalogue, pp. 583–84.

Fedotov, G.P., *A Treasury of Russian Spirituality*, London, 1952 [contains a very abbreviated version of the *Life of St Sergii* on pp. 54–83].

Ferrua, A., *The Unknown Catacomb: A Unique Discovery of Early Christian Art*, New Lanark, Scotland 1991.

Fink, J., *Bildfrömmigkeit und Bekenntnis*, Cologne 1978.

Florensky, P., *Iconostasis*, translated by Donald Sheehan and Olga Andrejev, Crestwood, NY 1996.

_____, *The Trinity–St Sergius Lavra and Russia*, translated by Robert Bird (Variable Readings in Russian Philosophy, n. 1), New Haven, CT 1995.

Giordano, S., *Die Hofkapelle im Normannenpalast*, Palermo 1984.

Grabar, A., "Un rouleau liturgique constantinopolitain et ses peintures," *Dumbarton Oaks Papers* 8 (1954), pp. 161–99.

_____, *Les revêtements en or et en argent des icons Byzantines du moyen âge*, Venice 1975.

_____, *La peinture byzantine*, ed. 2, Geneva 1990.

Hackel, A. A., *Sergij von Radonesh 1314–1392*, Münster 1956.

Klimenko, M., *The "Vita" of St Sergii of Radonezh*, Boston-Houston-New York 1980.

Kyslassowa, I., *Russische Ikonen des 14. bis 16. Jahrhunderts*, Leningrad-Düsseldorf 1988.

Lebedewa, Y.A. *Andrej Rubljow und seine Zeitgenossen*, Dresden 1962.

Mainka, R. M., "Zur Personendeutung auf Rublevs Dreifaltigkeitsikone," *Ostkirchliche Studien* 11 (1962), pp. 3–13.

_____, *A. Rublev's Dreifaltigkeitsikone*, ed. 2, Ettal 1986.

Marabini, C., *I mosaici di Ravenna*, Novara 1981.

Müller, L., *Die Dreifaltigkeitsikone des Andréj Rubljów*, Munich 1990.

Neubauer, E., *Kunst und Literatur im Alten Russland*, Düsseldorf 1988.

Nyssen, W., "Mysterium Trinitatis. Eine unbekannte Ikone der drei Engel bei Abraham vom Ende des 15. Jh. aus Nowgorod," in: *Drei Säulen tragen die Kuppel*, Cologne 1989, pp. 115–29.

Ouspensky, L.–Lossky, V., *The Meaning of Icons*, Crestwood, NY 1982.

Papadopoulos, S. A., *The Monastery of St John the Theologian. History and Art*, Patmos 1990.

Passarelli, G., *L'icona della Trinità*, Milan 1988.

Saltykov, A.., "Fragen der kirchlichen Kunst auf der Hundertkapitelsynode von 1551," *Hermeneia. Zeitschrift für ostkirchliche Kunst* 7 (1991), pp. 71–92.

Santini, P., *Santa Maria Maggiore: I mosaici del V secolo*, Rome 1988.

Schulz, H.-J., *The Byzantine Liturgy: Symbolic Structure and Faith Expression*, New York 1986.

Sergejew, V., *Das heilige Handwerk. Leben und Werk des Ikonenmalers Andrej Rubljow*, Freiburg 1991.

Smirnowa, E., *Moskauer Ikonen des 14. bis 17. Jhs*, Leningrad–Wiesbaden 1988–89.

Spitzing, G., *Lexikon byzantinisch–christlicher Symbole*, Munich 1989.

Stützer, H. A., *Die Kunst der römischen Katakomben*, Cologne 1983.

Vasiliev, A., "Andrei Rublev and Gregory Palamas" (in Russian), *Journal of the Moscow Patriarchate* 10 (1960), pp. 33–44.

Vzdornov, G. I., (ed.), *Die Dreifaltigkeit Andrej Rubljovs. Eine Anthologie*, ed. 2, Moscow 1989.

Weitzmann, K., *The Icon*, London 1978.

_____, (ed.), *The Age of Spirituality*, New York 1979.

Yablonsky, V., *Pachomii the Serb and His Hagiographical Works* (in Russian), St Petersburg 1908. Supplement: "The Life of St Nikon of Radonezh," pp. lxiv–lxxxi (Church Slavonic).